UNMASKING A NEW ERA OF CRIME

TODAY'S CAREER CRIMINALS AND CARTELS

Frank "Paco" Marcell

azpacomar@gmail.com

Editing by Cara Highsmith, Highsmith Creative Services, www.highsmithcreative.com

Cover and Interior Design by Mitchell Shea

I have tried to recreate events, locales and conversations from my memories of them. In order to maintain their anonymity in some instances I have changed the names of individuals and places, I may have changed some identifying characteristics and details such as physical properties, occupations, and places of residence.

ISBN-13: 979-8-9907720-0-7

eBook ISBN: 979-8-9907720-1-4

LCCN: 2024911268

Printed in the United States of America

First Edition 14 13 12 11 10 / 10 9 8 7 6 5 4 3 2 1

DEDICATION

To Alma, you gave me our children, grandchildren, and friends, and fifty years of your grace, mercy, and unconditional love.

"An excellent wife who can find? She is far more precious than jewels. The heart of her husband trusts in her, and he will have no lack of gain. She does him good, and not harm, all the days of her life."
— Proverbs 31:10-31 ESV

FOREWORD

I've known the author Frank "Paco Marcell" for almost 50 years. We were both working undercover narcotics when we met on the Mexican border with the United States in the 70's.

What he has written is based on his life and experiences growing up on the streets of Los Angeles in the turbulent 60's, his time spent in the jungles of Southeast Asia, years working drugs on the US-Mexico border, tracking and arresting gang members on the mean streets of Tucson and Phoenix, and working inside dangerous jails and supermax prisons in America.

Paco has earned an exceptional reputation with police officers, prosecutors, defense attorneys, and even hardened criminals as a "stand-up guy." He was the 24/7 go-to guy for information, intelligence, assistance, expertise, and backup.

Paco was the designer and catalyst behind the original Arizona Border Narcotics Strike Force, an intelligence-driven agency focusing on narcotics and organized crime information collection, analysis, and sharing. This is the agency that partnered with the FBI and took down Mafia boss Joe Bonnano. He was also the designer of the Arizona Department of Public Safety's nationally renowned GITEM unit that took on organized criminal gangs. Paco also developed and implemented the Gang Member Identification Criteria system to identify and track known and documented criminal gang members. These are just three of his passion-driven accomplishments that he boldly took on to make the streets of Arizona safer.

Paco is truly one of the foremost subject matter experts on career criminals and gangsters. His national reputation is from hard work, extreme loyalty to law enforcement, his friends, and the people he has chosen to serve for over 50 years.

Read this book, share it, and talk about it. It's not a "how-to" book. It's a book to cause you to think, be curious, and explore new and better ways to attack crime. The criminals you are up against aren't standing still, nor are they living on past laurels and doing things like they've always been done. Crime is their life; they are proud of it, and many are damn good at it. They've evolved and will continue to evolve. Hopefully Paco's book will help you stay alive and put more even criminals in jail.

Bill Richardson
Master Police Officer/Detective (Retired) Mesa Police Department, Arizon

CONTENTS

ACKNOWLEDGMENTS

The Lord, The Word, Alfa, and Omega—The Way, Truth, and Light. Dad, to the wise Colonel: Though you have long passed, you were the "one" who stirred me on the right path. You were always there for me. I have been forever grateful.

To my son, his fiancée, daughter, and son-in-law, brother, his lady, sister, and grandkids, I know I am blessed, loved and at times even tolerated. Your names will remain anonymous because of the reality of my written words and the contents of my journey.

To Arizona retired Gilbert Police Detective Stephanie Ameiss, this book would not have been finished without your technical assistance, patience, encouragement, loyalty, and counsel when I felt like giving up. Thanking you is not\enough. A true friend is a treasure.

Dr. Mary Lee Sheldon was my first (and only) English college professor. I sent you my manuscript to look over. You sent me back with wisdom, experience, and jewels that are now enclosed in my book. Your worldly insight is keen. You took a topic I expressed and broadened it to the real world. I am so grateful for our 50+ years of friendship.

To my long and loyal friend, retired police officers Bill Richardson, and author Dan Byram: I had you review my first thirty pages at the beginning of my writing. You gave back the "how" and "who" that helped launch the rest of the story. I needed the push that provided me with a vision of the potential future finish line.

Brian Parry, friend, author, and cop extraordinaire, I sent you a very raw manuscript to read. Never critical or demeaning, you offered your sound wisdom and encouragement about this writing game we have pursued. You have been a friend, a confidant for a long time. I am so grateful.

To all in criminal justice at all levels and in the military. Past, present, and future. You are brave and sacrifice beyond what the public knows.

Last and certainly not least Cara Highsmith curator and editor from Highsmith Creative. I found you through research that led me to Professor and author Marshall Terrell at Arizona State University. He was gracious to link us up for this project. You took my assorted, unstructured manuscript and made it into a readable format and much more. My very grateful appreciation.

> *"Sin speaks to the wicked deep in their hearts; they reject God and do not have reverence for him. Because they think so highly of themselves, they think that God will not discover their sin and condemn it. Their speech is wicked and full of lies; they no longer do what is wise and good. They make evil plans as they lie in bed; nothing they do is good, and they never reject anything evil."*
> — Psalms 36:1-4

INTRODUCTION

Before we get started, an explanation is due from the gate. You will find in the words ahead my outlook on crime, the career criminal, the American border as it relates to the Cartels, and episodes of my journey that form how I think and, most important, how I draw my conclusions. I tell you now that I did not approach my career on a personal basis as some kind of crusader. It was for a business, an occupation, and the *right* fit for me. Yes, I do look at things and situations as right and wrong, good and evil. I, too, am guilty of or have been guilty of the same things I detest and ask for forgiveness daily. We live in complicated, derisive times that polarize us. I try really, really hard to look at the world outside of my own perspectives, judgments, and wordy views. But I know I am short on doing so. I, like you, am a product of how I was raised, the things I have experienced, and the things I have witnessed and learned from. It is written that, in the end, we will find out the truth. For now, I hope somewhere, somehow, within my journey you will find something meaningful.

My name is Frank Marcell. For almost fifty years, most of my professional peers and associates have called me "Paco." Over the years, some have been curious and asked how I got that nickname. The simple answer is that around 1974 my fellow detectives started calling me that, and it just stuck for the rest of my career.

If you watch the movie Serpico and see a picture of me from that period, you might get a hint of how this tale has emerged. This is my story, and I'm sticking to it. It is a story about crime and the criminals that have confronted law enforcement. These are events that unfolded in Arizona, California, and New Mexico, over a four-decade period.

I grew up in the San Fernando Valley, California, in the 1950s and 1960s, a time of mixed cultures. Fast cars and low-riders, hot beaches and Hollywood. We drank Coors beer and cruised while listening to Wolfman Jack on the radio. Oldies, Do Wop, the Rolling Stones, and bluesman Jimmy Reed formed our soundtrack. "Evil weed" started showing up everywhere. Like everywhere. It was never referred to as marijuana. The thought was too foreboding, with legal consequences and social stigma. Coming from this environment greatly enhanced my understanding of the people who had opportunities to turn to a life of crime.

The Beginning of Understanding

For some three decades of my forty-two-year career in law enforcement, moving in and out of corrections institutions, I studied the behaviors of career criminals. In my final decade, I advised others across the United States about how career criminals think and why crime is their way of life; it follows a pattern that can be learned at an early age within our social structure. On a national level, the career criminal has the greatest derisive impact on the border, on local streets, and on life in jails and prisons.

The negative effect on our safety, security, and the costs of goods and services is not reported by political leaders, special interest groups, or national news media outlets. They tell you what they want you to hear. Even those who report strong support for local law enforcement do not analyze the economic and mental stress on society. As informed citizens, we must begin to read between the lines and voice a bold, unyielding leadership position to transform the criminal justice system; we, the voters, can make changes if we demand it. Acting to change a system begins with understanding the depth of the problem the opportunistic criminal presents.

My knowledge of their world evolved over years of dealing with individuals in their environments. It was a long and challenging journey to come to an understanding of the limits on local law enforcement departments. I spent much of my career at a supervisory level to work, mentor, and support the working troops, in the mix, on the streets, and in some notorious prisons and jails in the US. Why? I have studied the behaviors and stood face-to-face with many career criminals over the years. Most were members of organized criminal groups, including prison, motorcycle, and street gangs. A few specialized in robberies, burglaries, and drug deals—heavy-duty, tough individuals so feared they did not need to join a gang in or outside of prison.

In my career, I was blessed to think of the big picture and what could be done outside the box. I also enjoyed the hunt for people with bad intentions. Each lesson I learned made me better aware of problems in my surroundings. Thus, over the span of my career, I advised, authored, created, organized, and assisted in launching new intelligence and gang units on the streets and in state correctional and county jails. I authored several proposals or initiatives that became policy.

As I learned the behaviors of career criminals, I increased my responsibility as a criminal justice specialist to teach recruits and seasoned personnel what to look for and how to deal with dangerous individuals. The complexity of this expertise required me to prove the value of my credentials each time I was asked as a guest speaker and to each agency that hired me after retiring from the AZ DPS, always with an assigned task and expectation. You could say I became a fireman by putting out or containing fires through experience.

As a result, personnel in these facilities recognized the value of my work experiences and the threats within their incarcerated populations. They learned that there were offenders within their facilities who were so committed to criminal behavior, violence, and allegiances to gangs that it was necessary for justice organizations to adopt proactive measures, stricter policies, revised procedures, and innovative methods to maintain law and order and protect the public.

I wrote this book to share my vast experience after working in intelligence gathering for forty years. I spent a great deal of my life working to understand the career criminal's intentions. How does he think and respond to situations? What motivates him to behave in deviant ways?

I've authored and published articles on the topic of career criminals. In addition, I've been interviewed on television reality shows and have served as a guest speaker at many national conferences for police and corrections associations. The criminal trends I am witnessing today across America are too significant for you to ignore. In addition, my concerns about what might be on the horizon for law enforcement and the public compel me to share my thoughts now that I am retired.

My professional opinions are grounded in years of experience from field craft, interviews, encounters, observations, and crime statistics, patterns reported in crime research, and my instincts and spiritual insight. There is no better way to offer real evidence than to describe actual characters, their personal traits, and attributes—aspects that hold true today. These personality profiles and characteristics are ingrained in those who choose crime as a way of life. Examine them closely to know what to look for—discernible changes in mindset, make-up, and the characteristics of a new type of career criminal.

My observations and research derived from those who confided in me will help you understand their motivations. I noted some patterns and commonalities and ended up coining a term to refer to one of the groups: "The Opportunists"—career criminals responsible for new crimes sweeping the nation.

There's also a second group—the Mexican Cartels—who are responsible for a massive amount of criminal activity across our nation and the rest of the world. They have their hands in everything, and it's just downright alarming.

The experiences I relate in this book reveal a shadow—only a thin outline—of total criminal activity across the United States. My professional experience has given me razor-sharp insight into why and how criminals have come to control our streets, economy, and lives.

The following stories explain what these career criminals are capable of and are doing. They told me these stories to verify their long criminal histories. Their personal testimonies are a window into what we see occurring and into the future of America.

We will explore in great depth the career of a criminal that consumed a large portion of my life, covering all I know about them. I want you to know who they are and how they think. They are everywhere and anywhere, and committing crime is their main objective. I will share episodes from my career to exemplify and highlight a topic or circumstance. In a few instances I describe, there are a few words that may offend some; to this end, I apologize. In keeping it real, these are the words they would or have, or did say about the subjects I confronted.

My original intention was not to write a book to tell you why and how crime evolved around me. For me, writing a book was always for others. I would have preferred to be in the background and remain watching, hearing, and listening, less vulnerable. But I am old and experienced enough to know the stakes are too high to not cover these subject matters. This book will serve as a sort of library of my thoughts and experiences of the journey.

I hope to show law enforcement's efforts in fighting criminal gangs with an emphasis on the careers of two types of criminal groups and their crimes. I will cover the extent of criminal activity that, until now, you may not have been aware of. And by the time you finish this book and are somewhat aware, you might regret knowing.

Consider for a moment: Do you find yourself checking your surroundings more carefully when using the ATM? Do you feel secure finding a parking space in an unfamiliar location? Are you clutching your purse tighter, checking your wallet in a crowded location or while walking from your car to your front door? Once in a bank, do you pay closer attention to who's coming in?

If so, you are not alone. I also feel this, even though I've spent over forty years in law enforcement and corrections. I know I must be vigilant each time I go to the grocery store because my car may be stolen or, worse, I could become a victim of a carjacking. The unfortunate reality is that you are only as safe as your municipality's response time.

There is a type of emerging criminal, someone who follows a known pattern, that I call "an opportunist." I cannot unearth a more appropriate word to describe the mindset, patterned activities, and diverse types of people who recently have learned how to function criminally. These opportunists succeed in winning the war against local law enforcement as they operate within a social framework that actually reinforces bad behavior. I've identified two types of "Opportunist" criminals.

The first group involves individuals who are not necessarily criminals by nature. They simply take advantage of situations to take what they want. This happens when retail clerks are told by management not to interfere while stores are being robbed. Workers in stores selling fancy clothing, jewelry stores, convenience stores, etc. watch as looters take expensive merchandise, and they do not notify the police immediately. It is easier and safer for owners and employees to allow these opportunists to steal than to interfere. If these offenses remain unchallenged and unchecked, more young opportunists have or will become the new career criminals.

The second group is comprised of Mexico's cartels and the budding narco-terrorist threat, mainly along the US southern border with Mexico. Make no mistake; their presence, products are embedded coast to coast, spewing lethal drugs and related criminal activities across our public spaces into our schools, jails, and hospitals. They, too, are organized career opportunists.

It's time we pulled back the curtain and exposed them, along with the social structures that allow their behaviors to sicken us and weaken our economy and social fabric.

In the beginning, I put on paper a simple response regarding my concerns and frustrations with what I am witnessing today. I wanted to answer the question: *Why is such crime rising, especially in our largest urban areas and along the coastlines? Does the fault lie with local law enforcement or with a lack of reporting from the national news media and commercial cable channels?*

I wanted to provide a concise, updated revision of my previous career criminal assessments. I had intended to publish my responses individually in a law enforcement journal or local news outlet for public review. However, my initial effort had no impact; it was a cop-out. I quickly realized this subject is far too significant to limit the audience, considering current events. The only honest way I could put pen to paper was to recount my journey and share the story and the pathway to my conclusions. My objective is to provide authentic insight and offer genuine assistance to you, the reader.

From the beginning, I recognized that some would disagree with my analysis. You may even draw conflicting conclusions or misjudge my motives for pursuing this topic. That is your right, and I respect it. We are living in a divisive time. The fact that we are granted the liberty to disagree is a privilege. We can disagree and still enjoy the freedom of discussion while living in a democratic nation as great as America.

I hope my analysis answers lingering questions about the rising crime rates across America. Too often, the weak and the innocent are victims. Even those involved in crime eventually become victims of their own decisions. Citizens in a free society cannot function safely if crime is rampant. History depicts complex socio-economic reasons why great nations fall into decline; rampant crime and debauchery foreshadow decline, as we recall from stories about Rome, Europe in the 19th Century, and more recently, Central America. But we seldom speak about the apathy that was occurring in their citizenry. So, who is at the center of most crime today?

I began my writing with a broken heart a year after the passing of my wife, Alma. It was difficult to concentrate. I sat in my self-imposed solitary confinement, much like the criminals I talk about who were placed in isolated solitary incarceration. The past applause from public speaking and accomplishments—who I thought I was—all of that was gone, buried beneath layers of sadness. I recalled how my first college English teacher at Cochise Community College, Dr. Mary Lee Shelden, had previously encouraged me to write, so this writing and this journey were my way out of a dark place.

My dedication to the law enforcement profession and to helping the public remain safe are my special motivators. You can be assured that the decades I spent observing and speaking to criminals and then teaching others remain relevant today. Given the essentials of life in our complex world, crime affects people more than most understand. People do not want to live in fear, yet more people are questioning why crime is everywhere. They ask who is responsible. What can be done? Citizens sense this crime epidemic is spinning out of control as they watch a porch pirate grab a package at their front door in a neighborhood where crime was never a factor. I know this well; I have been a victim twice in recent years.

I have shared my frustrations and disappointments over the past few years as I have listened to news reports and read crime statistics. I understand what I am observing. I was in the game of watching career criminals for a long time. Yet I was second-guessing myself about what I saw happening across America until recently, in both rural and urban areas. Today, I see leniency by prosecutors, courts, and criminal justice systems that seem to be less engaged in appeasement and counseling instead of policing and protecting.

The police are obsessively scrutinized, devalued, and reduced when needed. They have become the villains of external socio-political forces. I wish it were not so. Changing the perceptions of the voting public concerning the role of our local police in preventing crime will take a bold, unyielding leadership transformation across local institutions, along with the tenacity of voters to demand it. Consider crimes you have observed in your neighborhood as I relate stories of opportunists and career criminals and their effects. What is crime costing us?

Regrettably, I call out in dread some leadership from the criminal justice system, from police to prosecutors, from court to confinement (prisons)—in many locales. Too many have retreated, but not by their own choice. I will tell you, in general, who is behind these decisions. But then it is up to you, in your area, to name names. To get this right, do not be swayed by some who present false crime statistics or by your predispositions and favored political news coverage. Do not be swayed by harmful and derisive race and reform agendas that separate us or by adhering to unyielding political party affiliation or point of view. This is not a "left vs. right" issue. Just look at the facts: crime and violence are everywhere and have become relentless. Please do not dismiss me as a fear mongering. Unfortunately, I know too well that some will not accept this premise until they or someone they know becomes a casualty of this reality and truth.

ABBREVIATIONS

AB	Aryan Brotherhood
ADCD	Arizona Drug Control District (Narcotics Strike Force)
APGTF	Arizona Prison Gang Task Force
AZDOC	Arizona Department of Corrections
AZ DPS	Arizona Department of Public Safety
BOP	Bureau of Prison
CITF	Correctional Intelligence Task Force
CGII	FBI/California Gang Intelligence Initiative
CI	Confidential source
CPGTF	California Prison Gang Task Force
CDCR	California Department of Corrections and Rehabilitation
DEA	Drug Enforcement Administration
DTOs	Drug Trafficking Organizations
FBI	Federal Bureau of Investigation
GITEM	Gang Intelligence Team Enforcement Mission
GMIC	Gang Member Identification Criteria
HUMINT	Human intelligence
ICPA	International Chiefs of Police Association
IGI	Institutional Gang Investigators
ILGIA	International Latino Gang Investigators Association
IOMEGA	International Outlaw Motorcycle Gang Association
ISU	Investigative Services Units
JIU	Jail Intelligence Unit
LC	The Los Carnales
NCO	Non Commissioned Officer
NMCD	State of New Mexico Corrections Department

NMGTF	National Major Gang Task Force
AZ NMM	Arizona "New" Mexican Mafia
MCSO	Maricopa County Sheriff's Office
OMG	Outlaw Motorcycle Gang
RICO	Racketeering Influenced and Corrupt Organization
SNM	Syndicato Nuevo México
STG	Security Threat Groups
SSU	Special Service Unit

THE PROBLEM

CHAPTER 1
THE STORY I WAS COMPELLED TO WRITE

I'm just a normal guy. I grew up in the rough-and-tumble town of Pacoima, California, 1950s-60s in an environment in which very few considered law enforcement for a career, at least with the crowd I hung around with. I'm sure famed actor Danny Trejo, who also grew up in Pacoima, would verify this. In truth, I now know it was the hand of a higher calling, the Lord, who guided and protected me throughout my life and led me into my chosen profession.

After World War II, my dad, still in the Army, met my mom while training new troops in the San Fernando Valley. They moved to a WWII veteran's housing project called Basilone Homes. Money was scarce then, but they were later able to move to Sunburst Street a few blocks south of Pacoima Jr. High. After a few years, knowing the Los Angeles freeway system would soon be encroaching, we moved to Arleta, then still Pacoima.

In my youthful days, I joined a rowdy, legendary car club that came mainly from San Fernando High School. We Anglos and Hispanics drove mostly low-riders and hung out at the Shoestring hot dog stand at Van Nuys Boulevard and Arleta Avenue in Pacoima. We would not back down from a fight as we roamed the San Fernando Valley, getting down with most all other car clubs in the San Fernando Valley. That was life in the 1950s-60s in Southern California.

As I recall, our car club had a mission. In our first gathering after school, we discussed the issue of bull-dogging harassment by school predators. We were bothered by how they were getting away with using intimidation tactics to take lunches or lunch money from innocent students who either could not or chose not to defend themselves. We took it upon ourselves to put a stop to this activity. (Perhaps the Los Angeles Police Department, Foothills Division, still has records showing how many times they responded to San Fernando High School during 1963-65.)

Many of us in the car club played high school sports; a few had dropped out of school to work, and the club included a few older fellows as well. We were not criminal-minded, at least during

the time I was involved, although some of our activities in the beginning to protect weak students against pred-ators may have been borderline unlawful. When we showed up at a party we just happened to hear about, we entered wearing our club jackets and vest. You could sense a chill in the air, an uneasiness, when we walked in as a group. More than predictable, someone would kickstart something, and the fight was on. Sometimes it's hard to distinguish between the predator and prey. Nothing has changed. That same group-think mentality exists in every club, mob, prison and street gang, or other nefarious organizations. When someone crosses a line, the battle is on.

My dad, a career military man, did not like my being involved in the car club. He was not overly strict, but he did not have to be—his bearing said it all. I never got busted or arrested, although there were close calls. I do attribute this to my dad; I never wanted to disappoint him, and I had a strong intuition to avoid trouble. I now know it was a higher calling—that the Lord protected me for my future career. I mention my high school club because it was training for working prisons and street gangs. We were not categorized as white supremacists, skinheads, *pachucos*, or *cholos* (names that arise in law enforcement training, in the news media, and in political labeling of ethnic groups). We were just a bunch of young dudes that clicked with each other. Though we were not a gang, nor did we think of ourselves that way, our core attitude and behavior closely mirrored what we might call a gang today. I'm sure this will surprise many who know me as an adult.

Our close camaraderie and friendship was like having many brothers. It was a great pull to be together; we backed each other up and could "be who we were." I know this same strong pulling exists for anyone who joins a gang. This same compulsion among juveniles needs more attention from counselors working with youth who find themselves in trouble.

However, I learned a valuable lesson from those youthful days hanging around with the fellas in the neighborhood that can occur in any setting—a club, a gang, sports team, school, workplace, military, or even church. There will inevitably be one who, for some reason, dislikes someone in the group. They may feel threatened by them and feel a need to belittle and dominate them.

Whatever the setting, you may think you are all brothers and sisters. You have come together as a team, working toward the same goal. But that "one" may be somewhere around. They may show their dislike openly or keep it close to the vest while sowing disfavor. These antagonists tend to come from two extremes. One is narcissistic and confrontational. This is the one no one wants to cross. They are not criminally minded per se, but they may exhibit a hidden criminal tendency that can show up at any time. In the extreme, they may resort to a physical confrontation, catching you unaware, unprepared, and ambushing you. It happened to me; I learned from it and never let it happen again.

The other type is submissive. They appear to go along with the program, but you can sense their discontentment. They may smile at you in open settings when others are around, but it's just a deception. I witnessed it back in the neighborhood and every place I have been since. They look for opportunities to undermine you behind your back.

4

Why do I share this? Because it's a story of life's lessons for many of us. In the end, it's not where you come from; it's how you end up. After graduating from high school and failing to attend college, I did a stint in the army. I jumped out of airplanes and did a tour in Vietnam. When I came home in 1968, things had changed; the old days were gone. Yet, my focus for a career was not fully established.

After several months of enjoying various kinds of entertainment and working in cement construction with a Mexican crew, I came to appreciate guys who work hard, really hard, all day long. But I knew it was time for me to move on and accomplish more in life. My dad, the wise colonel, advised me "to get out of Dodge," take advantage of the GI Bill, and try college.

Although I may not have wanted to hear it at the time, I knew he was right. It was the best advice I ever received. Without personal connections, I moved out to the Mexican border in Southeastern Arizona to attend Cochise College, a small, community, two-year college located between the small cities of Bisbee and Douglas. I became student body president of the college (who would have thought?), met a beautiful girl, got married, completed a college degree, began my law enforcement career, and never looked back. I had a new direction in life—a teenage boy's goal of becoming a police officer was becoming a reality.

The WHO of the Story

Full Disclosure: I possess no title as a forensic or behavioral psychologist. I do not possess a doctorate degree or teach at the university level, though I did complete a year of a master's degree program with no relevance to this subject matter. I am not a Federal Bureau of Investigation (FBI) Behavioral Analysis Unit graduate, although I wish I were. I do not belong to a research center or write for a news media organization. My political party registration is non-affiliated. I do not belong to an organized religious group. I keep my own council and personal faith. My ideology is not in the extreme far right or left. I believe in the rule of law, serving everyone equally and impartially . . . though, of late, I have concerns.

I am a realist and a pragmatist.

However, despite current concerns, I am profoundly grateful to have lived in a free country built on democracy and governed free of tyranny. I am truly blessed for the family and friends I have enjoyed all these years. They are not accountable for my findings.

This writing did not come easy for me. In August 2021, I lost my beautiful wife, my gift of fifty years, to breast cancer. The reality came suddenly, unexpectedly, cruelly, and so quickly she was gone. She was the best and most forgiving person I have ever met. Her walk with her Lord was steadfast. In my clumsy way of putting my thoughts on paper, she was my daily silent, yet present, editor who always encouraged me in every project. She knew my voice. She still does, and so, for months, I pondered how to start and what to say. My energy and enthusiasm diminished. But the combination of watching the daily news, along with emails and telephone calls from old peers who expressed their concerns about the crime epidemic, told me it was time to write! I needed to resurrect my previous accounts and explain what I see happening in America. Then, I remembered a quote that assured me of what I had to do.

> *"The world is a dangerous place, not because of those who do evil, but because of those who look on and do nothing."*
> —Albert Einstein (1879–1955),
> physicist and Nobel laureate

I knew it was time to write this southwest law enforcement history. So much has been written about the high inmate population and the types of crimes and criminals in the US, yet we are a nation that extols the virtues of personal freedom, liberty, and choice. We expect to be protected by a criminal justice system that is a guardian of democratic principles. However, democracies allow individuals and groups to make bad choices as well as good ones. The question is: "How can freedom from oppression sit side by side with individual freedom of choice to break laws?" The two aspects of our Bill of Rights appear inconsistent. So, I write in the hopes of providing you with an opportunity to consider this. By sharing bits of my life and career experiences, I aim to help you understand problems more clearly as you make decisions.

In 2010, I was asked to speak at an upcoming International Latino Gang Investigators Association (ILGIA) conference as a board member. I had not told fellow board members I was retiring for the second time. I felt it should be received in my thoughts by email. I wrote them a personal message expressing how difficult the decision was, given my devotion to my law enforcement career.

While searching through documents, I recently found a copy of the email I sent to my fellow ILGIA board members. I read a sentence that brought back memories I would like to share. "In communication, we often use an adage to emphasize what we are saying: I have truly been blessed in my career."

I had sent that email just as my California family was arriving in Phoenix from Los Angeles for the holidays. I had asked my sister to bring me our San Fernando high school yearbook from 1965, which I had not seen in forty years. Along with my graduation photograph was a caption that read, "Frank Marcell, future policeman." How many people can say they fulfilled their special youthful career dreams?

Throughout this book I will share personal stories and use real-life examples to emphasize the many lessons I learned in my career. Of all my dealings with career criminals, I can't recall more than a couple that were not involved with the illicit drug trade in some form. Things have not changed since my time of service; they have only gotten worse. I am not speaking of the casual recreational pot user. I am addressing the rampant addiction to an opioid or a stimulant drug. We now see this example multiplied by tens of thousands of people who have fallen into this trap. How long do we let this epidemic continue? What will it take to restore our citizens to health? Have we not seen enough to fund specialized drug facilities and hospitals? Are mental health personnel willing to work the streets to help bring in addicts and reduce consumption? Or is there a greater problem in our society behind a veil yet unknown?

CHAPTER 1 - THE STORY I WAS COMPELLED TO WRITE

Why are there such a vast number of people who have chosen this destructive way of life? Let's get serious: combating drugs has become a global problem. None of the federal agencies, singularly or collectively, can stop this war without a clear mission or position from political leaders. It is going to take a village, and all those in the village who care about the health of our youth and the next generation must work together in support. This will, of course, cost us financially. Do we want to make the investment? Does our financial investment in other countries take precedence over our own citizens?

At the local law enforcement level, police and prison guards are burdened with the results of the drug trade and the aftermath of associated crime on a daily basis. If that's not enough, law enforcement faces an increasing number of criminals willing and able to direct and control drug trafficking even while incarcerated. Peace officers at all levels refrain from acting on mandates from the authorities of higher governmental entities. Desperate times call for desperate measures.

But I submit the floodgate is open; there is no way to control the forces encountered by today's law enforcement officials. To help them, we must go forward with action at both the state and federal levels. Especially important is ending criminal activity along the US border with Mexico, and I believe the US Congress needs to pass legislation in accordance with Section 219 of the Immigration and Nationality Act to declare drug cartels as international terrorists.

As it stands, there is no ironclad method for combating organized crime and potential threats when

9

operatives freely cross national borders. We need to know who and where they are. The US does have experts who can optimize operational intelligence collection and tactical and strategic security-minded measures—professionals who work quietly, free from political expediency and utopian (global) idealism. And do it at great risk and sacrifice. My question is, "Why do we train the world's most advanced special operations forces from all military branches if we don't use them to protect our sovereignty at the borders?"

Yes, we are facing hard decisions. Our nation cannot remain risk-averse and believe we will live safely in a democracy. Our adversaries are powerful, sophisticated, shrewd, and relentless criminals and saboteurs who operate under their own rules. They are not curtailed by law. A selfish profit motive leads cartels or any other threat to tax immigrants crossing our border, to buy and sell children for sex and slave trade, and to kill millions of young people with illegal drugs. But I am most concerned with the unknown.

What I mention here is just the tip of their iceberg. They have made in-roads into legal or illegal enterprises involving corporations, land-title transfers, and fraud of government funds. Some elected offices may be unknowingly compromised by taking money for re-election without understanding how or why cartel affiliates or other deceptively corrupt groups have contributed those dollars. Dirty money paves the way for all illegal businesses and political decisions.

The impact of crime is measured in many different ways and, regrettably, to right a wrong may produce unforeseen consequences. As an example, recent measures restricting the prescription of opioid pain medication have been implemented. These were necessary measures as a consequence of unregulated pharmaceutical companies, fraudulent prescribing, and abuse by some in the medical profession. The irony is that we addressed the abusers while at the same time restricting a population that needs it the most: the geriatric population.

As the "graying of America" has expanded. Many elderly people live with constant pain, but they now find it difficult to get pain prescriptions for chronic health issues and special health needs. Doctors and drug providers must restrict prescriptions by law. While at the same time, illegal drug dealers are selling poison on street corners to addicts who are dying from overdoses daily. Such atrocities of appeasement may even be sanctioned by some government municipalities.

Because of these new restrictions and doctors' likely concerns about being scrutinized, many seniors now travel miles to purchase medication across the border in Mexico or Canada despite the potential dangers awaiting them there. Some use the internet to buy medicine that is packaged in China. These pills often do not contain the medicine the buyer paid for or the ingredients listed on the package not in the pills. We are compromising our priorities when senior family members have to resort to such hardships and potential danger.

The problems our seniors face are not directly related to career criminals, cartels, street gangs, or prison inmates. However, the indirect result is that the elderly are making choices for getting their medication that put them in great danger. Many reading this may find this topic distasteful or even fictional. Don't take my word for it. Ask any Customs Border Patrol agent who works the ports of entry and research the internet; you may be surprised to learn the extent to which this is happening.

As a culture, why have we made concessions and allowed crime and the criminal mindset to dictate even our health decisions? Why have we compromised and made concessions to crime and criminals that affect the welfare of others so close to our secure adobes, our places of rest, our businesses, families, and our places for recreation? Has a large segment of the population lost faith in the system and given in to fear of what they can't control? These are some of the questions we have to answer in order to see change.

My research and analysis come from my years of first-hand experience working as what some may call a "field subject matter expert." I say it has more to do with field matter experience. Knowledge comes from working in the arena, hands-on, or what in professional circles is called "lived experience." In the end, I was just a servant, doing the work I was meant to do. I hope some of it will provide readers with insight into how I see the future of crime and criminals evolving. In my home, I am looking outside and, at the same time, I am looking inside a country I care about deeply. I worked in the criminal and crime arenas as a career. So maybe I can now say I am in the car, the club, and the self I sought as a young man in the beginning of my career.

CHAPTER 2
LEARNING THE FUNDAMENTALS

When I reflect on my forty-plus-year career, like most of us, I recall specific events and memories and contemplate the long learning process the profession requires. What it took to get here was so much more serious study than my bachelor's degree could provide.

The committed career criminal world exists to make money through illegal gains. There is no limit to the range of tactics they use to achieve that end. They are not restricted to one particular activity; some resort to violence; others use fear and groupthink to take over and manage an action. Others use bribes or persuasion, especially with young, impressionable street gang members or other naïve individuals. Violence eliminates competition. Those in organized criminal groups take pride in being the most predatory.

They do not care about drug smugglers they hire who are arrested during a first attempt to carry illegal substances into the US. They do care about the occasional loss of money and drugs and will resort to other attempts to make up for the loss.

Leaders who are committed to lifelong criminal activity will always find innovative ways to make money. The committed career criminal has a dislike for long-term work commitments. They lack the work ethic common among law-abiding citizens. It is easier and faster to achieve profit through their own criminal activity or by persuading others they control to work the streets. Leaders become great risk-takers, void of concern for consequences. While pursuing a life of crime they dread the responsibility of the routine work environment that provides for themselves or for a family. Many find that confinement via incarceration frees them from the burden of daily labor. Even though they all seek release while incarcerated, many return to the same pattern of criminal behavior and are re-arrested, often for life.

The Legal Arrangements

Throughout their criminal journey, these men gain a solid understanding of the legal system. Some study law books and familiarize themselves with prior cases to avoid serious legal consequences—something they learn from their earliest years of incarceration, even as youths. You may have seen this reaction on crime reality TV shows. When contacted by police, the first thing they say is, "I know my rights," and they sometimes will even cite the elements of the criminal statute necessary for arrest pertaining to this situation. Some elite, seasoned criminals can afford expensive legal representation. They are prepared for such an event and use the ill-gained assets hidden in fraudulent financial accounts and, often, held for them in the accounts of others.

Less fortunate offenders rely on the appeals process to tie up the legal system. They may utilize the knowledge of a jailhouse lawyer for guidance. They intend to use the appeals process long enough to be offered a plea bargain, reduced sentence, or case dismissal. It would amaze most honest people to learn how often these appeals are won and a judgment is overturned from right in the belly of confinement. I don't recall who gave me this quote or where it came from; but I've had it for a long time, so I thought I would share it with you.

INMATE MOTTO
Admit Nothing!
Deny Everything!
Make Counter Accusations!
Demand Proof!
Ask For Continuances!
Make Appeals!
Lie!
And If All Else Fails ...
Sue The State

The Career Criminal Attitude

The most experienced and influential criminals avoid being discovered for their illegal activities by shielding their involvement from scrutiny. This is especially true if they are members of a prison gang or organized criminal organization. They orchestrate and direct others to carry out a particular crime or enterprise. Some of their "associates" serve willingly. Some are even family members. Others participate based on coercion, fear, or intimidation. While others view it as a status symbol. Amazingly, I have witnessed the level of control and influence one inmate of notoriety or status can have over an entire prison yard, numbering many, many dozens of inmates. They position them-

Alpha Dog

selves as the "Alpha Dog" in prison and out on the streets. They can also be non-affiliated, stand-up convicts who get the same respect. Those given this pass have their stuff together because they were respected by the right people, by influential people in their world, by bosses no one wanted to cross and earned the right of this status. They have and use their influences in many different ways. I use the term convict respectfully, just as it is perceived in the prison environment.

These men are more than inmates; they have earned the right to be convicts. Actor Danny Trejo, a former inmate who turned his life around several decades ago, is respected by many. In his book, *Trejo: My Life of Crime, Redemption, and Hollywood*, he explains his journey of redemption. Edward Bunker, now deceased, authored *Education of a Felon*, and he also achieved this status while incarcerated and on the streets before walking away from a life of crime. They, as some others, were able to find their calling outside of a life of crime.

There are no secrets in prison. The walls have ears that extend onto the streets, and storytelling builds legends. That means in my decades of working with prison gangs, conducting source interviews, doing research, while attending the CPGTF meetings and listening to countless stories by others, I learned a thing or two.

The Crime Inside and Outside

Once incarcerated, the career criminal will pursue crime as actively as he did on the streets. There is a lot of money to be made while incarcerated through various legal and illegal methods. Even more alarming is how much outside criminal activity on the street is directed from inside prisons and jails where the career criminal is in his environment.

In September 2022, the federal government announced its intent to hire eighty-thousand new Internal Revenue Service agents. I recommend they direct this new workforce to begin reviewing each income tax statement produced and filed by the incarcerated residents of every state and federal prison. They can also audit the scams executed through COVID-19 benefits, social security refund programs, and outside bank accounts, all conducted from within prison walls. The proliferation of these scams is overwhelming, and it is no secret within the corrections community that crime sometimes does pay. Spare the service workers this attention to earn a living, who waits on our table for a dinner night.

The Career Criminal and Other Adversaries

Hearing of so many officers involved in shootings within the last few years, I wonder if the suspects these officers are encountering are known by them before these encounters, if they are released prisoners continuing their careers with bad intentions. The career-minded criminal presents concern in the form of extremists and insurrectionists who may be alive on our city streets, ready to shoot out with any police officer he encounters.

As I assess incidents of police shootings across the US landscape, I wonder if law enforcement officers at all levels understand this increasing threat. Perceiving the extent to which local criminals are connected to powerful organizations and those under the leadership of imprisoned inmates is too overwhelming for new officers to accept; novice officers are not even aware this problem exists. Therefore, the consequences of criminal connections remain unknown. This also applies to policymakers and legislators who also lack awareness of the extent of these networks that plan crimes. They do not realize the internal national threat may connect incarcerated prisoners with on-going waves of street crime. Even those holding leadership positions in the criminal justice and intelligence communities with federal powers have not studied the reach and depth of this problem.

There is no "nice" way to arrest a potentially dangerous, combative suspect. The police are our bodyguards, our hired fists, batons and guns. We pay them to do the dirty work of protecting us, the work we're too afraid, too unskilled or too civilized to do ourselves. We expect them to keep the bad guys out of our businesses, cars and houses, out of our face. We want them to "take care of the problem." We just don't want to see how it's done.

Charles H. Webb, Ph.D., C.S.U.S

Permission received from author

On a national level, our history shows the US has confronted evil power brokers through two major world wars and multiple military conflicts. The Federal

Bureau of Investigations, Drug Enforcement Administration, and Alcohol, Tobacco, and Firearms departments, among others, have successfully undertaken major investigations to dismantle organized crime in the past. Prior Herculean efforts have ended national threats, but many today go unpublished and unknown to the public. These national defensive efforts are ongoing. The question is: How can the public learn the truth so voters can recommend resources and financial support? As civil servants, these heroic individuals' names remain largely unknown for their own protection.

But do we Americans have the will today as a nation to educate ourselves about the costs, both economic and social, that we suffer due to organized crime and the strength of criminal organizations? Lately, I have sensed an imbalanced criminal justice system, both local and federal—one that simply devotes too much investigation resources to social and political issues and incidents that are non-threatening, lack a criminal element, and are circumstances that only involve the low-hanging fruit. Should we, as taxpayers, not expect more from our paid state and federal authorities? Some will not agree with this, but I discern this is occurring, and many do understand.

The Career Criminal Mentality

Most, but not all, career criminals live their lives in a male-dominated, aggressive environment, in and out of jails and prisons, even while on probation or parole. Many have acquired a powerful survival instinct. They pick up an instinctive ability to size up and sort out who they perceive as weak in any surrounding. They, too, might be victimized by this perception by even more aggressive individuals. They find a spot in the pecking order.

All too often, they apply this sense of intuitive, misdirected thought to battling law enforcement, harassing correctional staff and the citizens they encounter in money-oriented commercial settings. Regrettably, this has often led to tragic encounters for victims on both sides. I learned that appearances can be deceiving, and sometimes a civilian trying to stop a robbery or theft takes on the wrong person and is killed. This is why managers of convenience stores tell clerks to just hand over the money and be allowed to leave rather than risk their life trying to take down a criminal with a knife or gun.

Many years ago, a young officer in a sister city outside Phoenix patrol initiated a routine traffic stop. He did not know that the driver was an Aryan Brotherhood member recently released from prison. The ex-inmate was strung out on crystal meth and resolved not to go back to prison. As the officer approached the vehicle, he noticed a female passenger, and the driver quickly exited the vehicle wearing a trench coat. The officer's instinct told him something was wrong and he immediately conducted a pat down, which revealed a .45 caliber in a shoulder holster, and the fight was on. After a struggle, the officer got the suspect on the ground and called for backup when the suspect yelled to the girl, "Shoot him, shoot him." As the officer turned to look toward the vehicle, he saw the female occupant crouching, pointing a weapon at him. The officer immediately drew his weapon and fired, terminating this accomplice's threat and her life.

In this case, the offender was given a lengthy prison sentence and spent many years in the Special Management Unit, isolated from the general prison population. He was eventually released from prison, and he is now back in society. His actions directly resulted in citizens becoming heavy drug users strung out on methamphetamines. Since his release from prison, I have spoken with him, discussed our mutual roles, and discussed the changes he has gone through. I am told he is now striving to live free from crime and is haunted by his life from his many years in solitary confinement. I only wish him well, and I hope he can put crime behind him.

The Contempt for Authority
Most career criminals hold authority figures in disdain. This dislike and mistrust is a learned behavior. Youths learn it from listening to the men in the family or other respected persons who display resistance to authority figures. The emotion of fear and contempt is passed down from generation to generation via stories of conflicts with cops to show how they gained and gamed over authorities and other influential cultural figures. This ingrained, established communication permeates whole neighborhoods of all ethnic communities, even schoolyards.

Anyone in authority, from a teacher to a peace officer, is someone these youths learn not to trust and not to talk to about trouble. Unfortunately, as he mixes with groups of his own kind, the untrusting, naïve young person is left to deal with this deep-seated defiance alone with no one to talk to, except their peers. It is difficult to go alone against the will of the group. He decides that rules and restrictions do not apply to him. By the time the police intervene (perhaps following a simple theft at the Circle K), the path to criminal behavior is under way.

Juvenile offenders often show contempt to a store owner or authority figure by using aggressive behavior and threatening words. This kind of youthful offender can react with hostility over the slightest perceived provocation, especially if he feels someone has disrespected him or his friends. This anti-social behavior is significantly heightened under the influence of drugs or alcohol. For many youths, such use of "macho behavior" is a mark of bravado, a signal of loyalty and commitment within the peer community. Therefore, information on a youth's family/peers and ethnic background is important to a correctional/law enforcement official while there is still hope to steer an adolescent away from a life of crime.

Many career criminals, terrorists, and revolutionists have a propensity for sudden physical, uncontrolled violence or rage. Men who have worked their way through their beliefs, the jail to prison system, or who belonged to a prison or street gang use violence for power and self-protection the group offers them. This also applies to those raised in an ideology of hate toward other cultures or religions. Having observed violence at home and rage in the community, they consider loud, overt violence a normal reaction to conflict. They commit crimes deliberately, during or following special events, and are planned, calculated, rational actions. They know what they are doing; the result follows what they learned as they were being schooled in their culture and surroundings.

One night, while brushing my teeth, a clear thought came to mind. The inner voice said, *Use caution when describing criminals; do not paint all who run afoul of the law with a single brush.* I knew what this message of caution meant. Because I dealt with prison gang members for a long time, violence was often a means to an end, as they described in the interviews. I became acclimatized to thinking of most criminals as one group. It is true that some career criminals purposely avoid violence at all costs; they have a neutral view of the police yet they are caught up in an endless game of incarceration.

There are others who lack a predatory nature or mistrust of authority, for many of them "doing time" can be a scary experience. An example may be people who are imprisoned for lesser drug or driving offenses, for an act of theft, for fraud offense: all mostly for non-violent crimes. These inmates face a predatory environment following incarceration. The system of confinement is just too big to separate all sheep from wolves. There is no other way to put it.

The Fascination with Weapons and Shootings

Hardcore, defiant career criminals have a fascination with weapons. They most always keep a gun nearby, most illegibly obtained. While in close contact, some prefer using wedge weapons, like a knife. A 'shank' (knife) in prison is like a shotgun for a homeowner for protection. How is this possible within a prison? They have no access to handguns in prison, yet they find ways to "make a weapon" that serves as a blade. Many who engage police in a shooting situation have spent years incarcerated, so are they prepared to use a lethal weapon. The days of getting down and 'throwing blows' one on one to settle a dispute seem to be long gone. The way criminals target officers is the single greatest liability to law enforcement upon contact or during an arrest.

Few are military veterans or trained shooters, so they do not have a great deal of familiarity with a variety of legal weapons. They may practice using a handgun or long gun in some obscure shooting location, but they know they are prohibited from openly possessing or purchasing a firearm. How often have you heard on the evening news that a career criminal or disturbed individual was involved in a shooting? Do you wonder where he got the weapon? Did he make it from a kit, buy it at a gun show or online, or simply steal it? A criminal intent on obtaining a firearm will do whatever it takes—just as the heroin addicts will- to score his next fix.

Untrained shooters use the "point and shoot" method: aim, point, shoot quickly, and have the mind-set to flee! This method of shooting is instinctual and can be very accurate. This leaves the shooter's mentality free of pre-training peace officer methods and restrictions and can be quite precise in close-quarter situations. Remorse and consequences are not part of their pre- or post-mental attitude or conditioning. Law enforcement officers, to the contrary, are required to train with a weapon and learn how and when to use it, as well as follow strict guidelines and policy procedures. But it is in an environment free from stressful and violent situations. In many spontaneous and forced shootings, the officer is not thinking about the methods that are taught on the shooting range to qualify to carry their weapon while on duty. It is a life-and-death situation. This "point and shoot" technique sadly occurs against innocent, compliant store clerks when a criminal plans a robbery or other crimes as well. And in some cases, the mere possession of a weapon is not enough; the act of shooting an innocent victim only emboldens them.

The Group Think

During incarceration, inmates align themselves with groups or cliques of their own kind for survival The group operates by force or cunning. There are not a lot of choses in prison environments. As a result, groups of ethnic inmates can offer protection, and continue their criminal enterprises even wh le incarcerated. However, whatever their race may be, they often put aside animosity to conduct or further their illegal business purposes.

New street gang members who come into an adult prison system for the first time must learn how to obey the "convict code." They are undisciplined and full of bluster. The things they did on the streets amongst their peers do not apply in a prison environment, and the slightest provocation or disrespect against another race or group within the prison system could kick off a serious racial conflict. There is always a silent tinderbox of emotions in the air in many prison systems, both state and federal, and the slightest perceived disrespect could result in a major confrontation putting the prison staff at risk.

This is why the Federal Bureau of Prisons and most state departments of corrections have adopted Security Threat Group Unit policies. Unfortunately, security threat groups are a magnet for up-and-coming young inmate career criminals. It is a step-up for them in their criminal pursuits. They are predatory and responsible for many illegal activities and assaults committed in prison. The group member puts forth efforts to rationalize or minimize a crime; he attempts to manipulate the judicial system. Perhaps he is already a student of legal proceedings who can skillfully use appeals, writs, and the subpoena process to their group's advantage. They communicate information across the group to help save a fellow member.

The overriding trait of these like-minded career criminals, members of power groups, is commitment. Upon release from prison, most will continue to prey upon the community from which they originated—their own ethnic group—continuing to dare those who oppose them. Nationally, the violence and notoriety attained by these security threat groups have prompted law enforcement agencies to proactively create special enforcement units to target their activities in those communities and places they frequent.

Leading into 2024, news media accounts have suggested that some south and Central American countries have opened their prison doors during our current open border policy. If this is true, many will be hard-core gang members of their country of origin. They will follow a path to existing gangs and establish gangs of ethnic origin and mindset within many urban and rural cities across the US. In the last couple of decades, federal and state law enforcement task forces have worked tirelessly to curtail their vast criminal activities. Sadly, much of these efforts will be in vain, as the influx of vast numbers will be overwhelming in the near future, if not already. To penetrate these gangs is difficult, and they come to the US with a different mindset—they have no regard for our laws. They are distrustful of outsiders, stick together, and use violence as their trademark indiscreetly to establish territory and epitomize the group. A storm is brewing.

The Threat They Pose

Generally, when law enforcement, corrections, and researchers attempt to assess organized criminal groups, it is common to focus on group behavior instead of profiling individual members' influence and behaviors inside the group. It is most often the singular individual who poses the greatest threat and because of their influence within the group. Knowing individual criminals' profiles, backgrounds, characteristics, and traits is paramount to officer safety. This is especially important for undercover personnel or for anyone conducting an arrest or search warrant. It is also helpful in assessing criminal activity trends or patterns across a jurisdiction.

Bad guys with bad intentions tend to cluster in certain areas, and they follow learned patterns. Therefore, clinical psychoanalysis of a career criminal's personality will vary broadly. Validated Analysis is best left to professional clinicians. The review of an individual's history of past behavior and violence potential, however, does show how he thinks; this is important to predicting capabilities in future confrontations and crime patterns.

Numerous significant events in Arizona have involved career criminal members or associates of Security Threat Groups. Sadly, some incidents have injured or killed law enforcement officers. It is reported more frequently now that police and corrections officers are being shot at, assaulted, and caught unaware, and endangered in routine situations across most cities. In every contact, things can turn bad and unfold in seconds, resulting in the use of force. These confrontations happen during traffic stops, while delivering search warrants, and during every other conceivable encounter with predatory criminals. The career criminal has no boundaries. Career criminals come from every race and ethnicity and survive in every location, urban and rural.

They prefer to reside in communities that allow them to pursue activities unnoticed. Arizona is a prime location because of its border with Mexico and its access to drugs. Criminals eager to master the smuggling business learn of these "safe locations" as places with opportunities. They get the messages from other like-minded criminals. Often, they travel regularly to a new location to avoid police scrutiny; they may try to blend into a new environment by attending local functions and socializing with citizens who may not know their background or remain in the shadowy world surrounded by like-minded individuals.

The Survival Skills

Career criminals have an acute awareness of their surroundings. This is a learned trait tied to an inflated ego. This was the case with the AB we arrested in the Meth-House I mention in another chapter. He, like many, was conditioned to size up the arrest situation quickly and take action, if necessary, using fear, intimidation, and cunning for his own self-preservation. The threat and use of violence is one way to secure the way out of a situation, similar to what our military has encountered in jungle and urban conflicts even till now. People with bad intentions are survivors so they get to know their surroundings before deciding on an action.

Like minded criminals and adversaries learn combat/survival skills in the streets, in jail, or by living in a violent home, and environment at an early age. By reviewing criminal histories, I recognized a multitude of different crimes, i.e., armed robbery, burglary, narcotics, assault, etc. that were common in the repertoire of violent criminals. They switch gears quickly into a threatening mindset even feeling a false sense of invincibility; this makes them all the more dangerous. In such a situation, my findings and experience show if they chose to shoot, they are usually successful.

They also learn the survival skills of tolerance and deception. To forego a violent situation, come under suspicion, or for the purpose of manipulation. They can be charismatic, charming, and complimentary. These types of attributes may show up to extricate themselves from a situation or to further pursue or compromise an unwitting person. They have already made up in their mind about what they would do.

The Seizing Up-Stare Down
During police contact, in a correctional setting, or in a public place, citizens do not realize that career criminals constantly scrutinize them. The career criminal thinks he is smarter than the average citizen, so he attempts to use techniques to manipulate every encounter. A favorite power play is the stare-down, an intimidation tactic that puts fear into most people. In prison, the inmate uses the stare-down to see if the officer(s) they confront or fellow inmate will break eye contact or back away. To look away is a sign of weakness. An officer cannot tolerate backing down; he needs to tell the inmate he knows the tactic. The everyday citizen, however, is wise to simply ignore or walk away from a stare-down. For the average, unprepared citizen to acknowledge or confront someone trying to intimidate them, it could instantly result in physical violence.

The Female Agenda
Some may be thinking, Are female career criminals also? Unfortunately, yes. Our state and federal correctional facilities are filled with repetitive female offenders who, like their male counterparts, have chosen a criminal lifestyle. Most are imprisoned for drug-related offenses, but their crimes have no bounds. They exhibit many of the same characteristics I have described in males. Might you ask, can a

female become a prison gang member? No, I know of no exceptions; to my knowledge, the prison gang is an exclusively male-dominated organization. Folks have previously written much with greater experiences than I about dealing with female offenders.

Yet, it is important to note that women do play a significant role in facilitating and coordinating drug conspiracy with incarcerated male members and others out on the streets. The women are committed to and loyal to their incarcerated male counterparts. They are skilled at multitasking and often possess a high degree of self-taught business knowledge, handling multiple inmates' requests, finances, and arranging clandestine meetings.

In recent times, I've seen a different profile of female criminal offenders. From news media accounts I have learned, they appear to be less criminally minded but inclined to be more opportunistic and brazen, showing a total disregard for authority or victims. They engage in theft, store looting, vandalism, and drug use openly with undaunted consequences. Those involved with a career criminal male counterpart can act as a trained observer, carrying messages and often weapons or drugs in and out of a correctional facility and on the streets.

Although I certainly came across females while working narcotics with street and prison gangs or other assignments, they were not a major priority in my career. However, I did have two female sources; one had close ties to an Aryan Brotherhood inmate. I met her through a parole officer. The other was a family associate with the Arizona "New" Mexican

Mafia; I never met her in person. She acquired my work telephone number from another parole officer. For a couple of years, both were great sources who provided me with current activities and personal information on members I would not have known otherwise. In time, both stopped calling, and I never heard of their fate.

I recall participating in a massive search at the AZ DOC Perryville prison west of Phoenix that swerved as the women's complex in around 1986. I expected just another routine task, but was I surprised? As we approached the cell block for a search, the female inmates became loud, boisterous, uninhibited, and nasty with no restraints. I admit it; some of the suggestions they offered made me a bit uncomfortable. *Smile*. I was relieved to return to work in a male prison setting.

The Act of Revenge

The psychology of revenge is greatly underestimated when identifying motives for mass casualties and multi-victim criminal atrocities. The murder of a store clerk during a robbery is, however, different from the shooter involved in mass shootings in public places like elementary schools or a blitz-krige-style rape and murder. Individuals with twisted emotions and ideologies shoot to avenge a wrong and inflict other forms of pain and suffering. They target schools, malls, and public events for publicity, as well as citizen's homes.

They stake out local or distant targets prior to murdering innocent victims. They always calculate and plan their acts and often will voice an act of revenge, leave a message on social media, and blame society for a grievance or personal dissatisfaction. Individuals closest to them will be the first to hear what is playing out in their thought process. Gun owners must be aware of individuals who appear uneasy or deceptive while purchasing a weapon. This same observation applies to other situations, for example, those practicing at a gun firing range or who act nervous while sheepishly looking over weapons at a gun store. When we become aware of the dangers that anti-social individuals suffering from a mental disorder pose, we are better able to notify an authority who can intervene to investigate the person.

From messages on social media and expressions of revenge, we realize that many prospective mass murderers give themselves away before the traumatic event. What is disturbing about a mass shooting situation is the fact that the public is not more involved in notifying authorities when they suspect an individual could be dangerous.

The disturbed individual usually leaves verbal, written, or video communication explaining his or her dissatisfaction. It is critical that anyone who reads or hears of such a message state their personal grievance. Statements of violence and announcing a potential shooting should contact an authority who can immediately profile the individual. Given the number of mass casualty shootings in the last decades, citizens must learn to intrude when one's conscience tells them something is wrong. The old saying is, "If you see or hear something strange, say something to someone"—to save children and fellow citizens.

However, common sense, caution, and discernment are required to know the difference between someone pissed off at someone, something, or an event and someone verbalizing or exhibiting plans with a violent, destructive outcome.

Over time, I have come to realize, having witnessed the frequency of mass shootings, that there is an innate, intrinsic conditioning within each of us that does not want us to believe that the person we think we know, consider a friend or a family member, is capable of such a destructive event. Therefore, we are preconditioned to believe that the action of notifying someone in authority of our concern is an act of disloyalty and even betrayal.

The US has undergone a radical change within the last few decades: the quick fix of technology and social media. An increasing barrage of causes related to COVID-19—environment, race, gender, wealth, power, recognition, and unrelenting global military conflicts—have reshaped our moral compass. We are a nation weary, restless, and distrustful in search of peace, yet we are acting out with rebellion that has spawned wanton revenge, resulting in unforeseen casualties and criminal behavior.

Dangerous Criminal Encounters

In the mid-1970s, on two different occasions, I worked with Drug Enforcement Administration (DEA) Agent Hector Berrellez, author of the Amazon series and book *The Last Narc* that resulted in shootings. Hector was the undercover agent for drug buy-busts-walk. Fellow DEA Agents, Detective Frank Gonzales with the Cochise County Sheriff's Office and I were his backup team. One bust occurred across the US border in Naco, Sonora, Mexico, after dark in an old neighborhood on a back dirt road behind two old adobe buildings. I don't recall the particulars of what led Hector to the Mexican dealer across the border, but I do recall how it went down. Hector and another DEA Agent were to meet the seller in front of a home, where they would negotiate by Hector's undercover car. Because to my recollection it was a buy-and-walk situation, we did not expect problems.

Hector's long game plan was to buy up to a high quantity and eventually lure the seller to the US side where he could make an arrest, and perhaps lead him to people higher up in the distribution chain. Hector parked his car as planned and we, his backup surveillance team, found a spot down the street where we had a visual of Hector's car. We could not get too close for fear of getting noticed, burning the deal.

Two Mexican men met Hector at the front of his car. Because of our distance, low lighting, and darkness, it was difficult to see what was happening. It appeared to us that they were having a lively conversation. Suddenly, the four started walking towards the house. We knew this was not part of the game plan; we asked ourselves, "Could this be a rip-off?" Concerned, we left the car quietly and walked to the house. As we approached, looking between two old adobe homes into the backyard, we saw Hector and his partner standing there, but we could not see the two Mexican banditos. In a flash, Hector's partner fell to the ground, and at the same time, shots rang out.

Hector already went for his gun. We started running towards Hector; many shots were exchanged. When we reached Hector, all was quiet; we noticed one of the dealers several feet away on the ground had been shot, but alive. The other one was standing nearby, holding his hands up.

We were told Hector's partner had tripped over a tire, but he was okay. Hector told us to get back across the border to Arizona; he would deal with the Mexican Judicial Police. I cannot tell you what later occurred. Hector did not mention this incident in his book, nor did he include the next incident that occurred while he was undercover. However, if you know Hector, you would not be surprised to hear that he beat or as fast as the bad guys to the draw.

The other case occurred at a park just before dusk in Bisbee, Arizona. Hector was negotiating for a large quantity of amphetamine pills. A few of us were posed as his backup team. Just before the meeting with the dealer, we received a telephone call from a source advising that the dealer would be armed. The subject showed up alone; he showed Hector the pills. When Hector identified himself as the police, the suspect drew his weapon and fired. Several shots were exchanged, and the suspect started running through the park. DEA Agent Tory chased him. The suspect's head met the fate of the agent's revolver. The lesson learned by the bad guys is: don't shoot at the police. They are armed and trained in weaponry.

These two examples highlight the thinking of those involved in criminal activity when they come up against trained undercover officers. The criminals had obviously preconceived notions of how they would respond if confronted. But then, so did the police. To reinforce the seriousness of this kind of situation, I remind readers that I conducted interviews with career criminals who had prior convictions for gun violations. I've asked them specific questions about their mindset during a crime. Using different scenarios, for example, I might ask, "While doing an armed robbery, if police arrived, were you prepared to use a weapon?" or "Had you already made up your mind, you would shoot it out with police if you felt you could get away?"

The answer on several occasions was "yes." They were prepared to use a weapon, if necessary. Remember, their survival is a way of life in crime. They don't fake it. Some are so committed; they use whatever is at their disposal at the moment: a gun, a knife, or their fists. Their determination is to escape. They use violence to settle scores. The thought of injury and pain does not deter them. Many grew up street fighting in hostile environments, so they know pain; they have used a knife or a gun for protection. They are not, on the whole, afraid of the police and will take on any force applied to restrain them.

The Realistic Boundaries and Encounters

Officers recognize that not all criminals we encounter will comply with a command. When the job gets complicated, it turns ugly in a way that few outside law enforcement understand. Law enforcement officers are now videotaped, and their actions are scrutinized after the fact, mainly by the media. As hard as officers may try, not all violent encounters can be resolved by police community relations committees, persuasion, or by elected officials who think policing techniques can be learned in a psychology class.

Police, corrections personnel, and most citizens are not trained in various combat styles such as Mixed Martial Arts (MMA) or down and dirty street fighting. Officers should learn MMA so they can restrain a combatting suspect quickly to stop a physical altercation. Because most officers may lack certain MMA skills, we see videotapes from a crime scene showing multiple officers swarming a suspect. Even with such training, group force may be needed to stop the threat and restrain a person during an arrest: (see the picture of such an arrest from the Internet.) The "cop swarm", in hand-cuffing and arresting a suspect on the ground, is a misfortunate appearance, often perceived as over-kill—police brutality. In reality, it may prevent injuries to the police and offenders. Conversely, the general public and news reporters do not know that career offenders are willing to take on the police and use a hidden weapon; career criminals expect the "cop swarm"—they take it in stride—it is what it is.

The Observable Signs

In a law enforcement career, you more than likely will encounter an individual prepared to challenge you, or someone predisposed to use violent tactics and actions. There are observable signs you will spot quickly if you know what to look for so you are prepared to react. These signs may apply in a shooting encounter, a seemingly normal routine situation, or a covert assignment. There are those with far more expertise than I, but I offer you a few of the observable signs I have picked up along the way. The subject's face will bear a look of serious determination as if he was instantly sizing up and measuring the environment. He will appear immediately uptight, offended, or nervous when a situation does not require such emotion. Their eyes may be wide and focused directly on you. Their breathing may be accelerated.

However, the opposite may hold true as well. They may well be assessing you to determine their best plan of action. You may also encounter someone who initially looks calm but immediately tries to intimidate you. They are looking to determine your instant reaction. The goal is to try to back you off from pursuing any further action. At the moment of contact, they might quickly look around in a sweeping motion to see who is around or to decide where it is safe to escape.

They may act like they do not hear you in these scenarios and ignore your commands. They are stalling, assessing what they should do next. They may even be showing you their hands without your command. Usually, their hands are not high in the air but held at waist level, palms facing you. But this is only a ploy. They believe they can get to their weapon faster than you can get to yours. That is why they often conceal their weapon in the front or back inside their pants, in other clothing, or in a vehicle located at arms-reach.

They might also determine if they can overpower you with physical force. All these actions are not normal human behavior. There exists a high likelihood they might be under the influence of drugs or alcohol or suffer more serious concerns. Have they just committed a crime? Are they in possession of a weapon or drugs? On parole, or have outstanding warrants?

Finally, they might have decided they just did not want to go to jail so they will do whatever it takes to commit the crime and flee.

If your instincts tell you this is happening, don't second-guess yourself; remember, you are not alone. Do not hesitate to call for assistance. We are all humans and want to go home at the end of the day. Do not put yourself in harm's way by thinking you have everything under control. There are some situations that may require additional help.

Regrettably, such encounters are not limited to criminal justice personnel. The unsuspecting store clerk or bank employee might also become a victim of this offender's pre-planned mentality, with no regard for or remorse for the victims he may kill or injure. It is happening in neighborhoods once considered safe, far too frequently. Citizens are asking, "What is going on?"

Becoming aware of a potential life-threatening criminal response requires awareness, vigilance, and discipline during contact situations. We all must remain aware of our surroundings. A good rule for officers to follow is "approach determines response." Does your body language reflect confidence? Are you focused? Do you project what you say and believe what you say in your commands? Sometimes, this is all that is necessary.

Every young officer who enters the criminal justice profession and advances through the ranks experiences a method of introspection. Most people don't understand the difficult process a peace officer learns as they advance through several branches of service.

As a novice, it begins by filling out an extensive historical background application, followed by a written examination, a physical fitness test, an oral board interview, and a background investigation, and many agencies require a polygraph test. After successfully graduating from an academy, most survive a six-month field probationary evaluation to determine if they are cut out to be a peace officer. All who succeed and finally wear a badge share pride in their achievement. Do some slip through with personality flaws that cause authorities to remove them from the profession—naturally? This is the case in all professions. In a crisis situation or moment of temptation, the hidden human personality is unmasked.

Try to imagine what it's like to follow a known criminal in a patrol car or even an officer wearing plain clothes driving an unmarked undercover vehicle. He has to conduct a traffic stop. There are many scenarios to draw from—you pick one. If necessary, turn on your blue light and siren, and the vehicle will not stop. Suddenly, the driver quickly accelerates to unsafe speeds, ignoring all traffic signs or safeguards for other motorists. This is a moment no officer wants to be confronted with-The vehicle Pursuit

Your mind is racing, and your adrenaline is pumping as you ask yourself why he didn't stop! If it's not for a stolen vehicle, bad license plates, or expired tabs, what is it? Your safety and the safety of on-coming traffic are foremost; many things are rushing through your mind! Is the subject under the influence, a fugitive from justice, has he just committed a crime, is he holding drugs, and is he armed? You may be alone, awaiting backup.

The danger is increasing; you feel a flood of emotions and questions you are asking yourself. You only have two hands. One is holding your radio by a cord to your car radio. You're talking with dispatch, continuously calling out speeds, traffic conditions, safety concerns, and locations. You can't take your eyes off the road ahead as you weave in and out of traffic. You're thinking, "I can't lose this vehicle; stopping this crime depends on me!" You're thinking, "How is this going to end?" You know, deep down inside, it could be bad, really bad, and even deadly.

Today, the chase is viewed and recorded by every witness with a cell phone. Some observers quickly blame a peace officer for every outcome and later give the evening news reporter a negative opinion. This is the reality on the streets. Behind prisons and jails, our responsibilities and anxieties became greater in a close custody, high-security setting. You are outnumbered, you do not carry a weapon, and most people you deal with do not respect you.

Each increasingly responsible assignment allowed me to gain experience specializing in working-career criminals, so my confidence grew. Every officer's preceding assignment gave them credence, making them feel unflappable and eager for the challenge. When it came time to execute a search warrant, the word was, "let's go! Do you need an undercover officer?" A few hands of volunteers would go up to take down a "bad guy" we knew was armed. We learned to move in faster and quicker. The day-to-day work was one incident and one arrest at a time, singular in thought and action.

CHAPTER 3
THE PREDICAMENT OF MODERN POLICING

Criminal justice theorists, politicians, and the public have forever debated who it is they want to police and how to go about doing the job. In the last few decades, the process for the recruitment, application, and background process of those seeking employment in law enforcement has never been stable. I suspect that is the case in federal agencies as well.

From the late 1960s-70s, many who found employment policing our streets were cut from a different cloth. I do not judge this good or bad. It was part of the times we lived in. Some officers were perhaps less educated. Their numbers included scores of veterans, some returning from the Vietnam War. Some were local men who sought a different kind of adventure. Some were blue-collar workers seeking greater benefits; some were citizens who sincerely wanted to improve their neighborhoods and make a difference. Countless others came from diverse environments and backgrounds, from middle class, racially mixed cultures. Some of these young recruits came from an environment in which disputes were settled shrewdly and swiftly, using fists and the same neighborhoods as those who ended up in a life of crime . . . peers from school.

As a part of this era's recruitment, leaders were recognizing that some new recruits exhibited more of a predatory and prey behavior, or a sheep-to-sheep-dog mentality, as protectors. Many of these recruits' home environments prepared him to deal with peers who were ingrained in criminal intentions. The hiring process prior to around the 1990s was more forgiving of past minor discrepancies or minor offenses. A person's home neighborhood, cultural background, and finished public education were less critical and more acceptable than a formal higher education, the assets the new recruit brought to the job, especially military training.

Around the 1990s, a different philosophy of policing, hiring, and accountability became the norm. Emphasis and priority went to recruits with a college degree, specifically in criminal justice. A young recruit's background had to be sterile, clean of past missteps or drug use. Even experimental smoking weed as a youth or in college could disqualify a candidate. It became increasingly difficult for a middle-of-the-road person to enter the law enforcement workforce. I personally knew a few candidates who were bumped who I thought would have been excellent officers.

All the while, the environment and surroundings on the streets of crime and violence were still the same. There are still people who will hurt a citizen for illegal gain. These criminals, worthy foes, many with skills learned on the mean streets. The image of the police today is less positive than it was before, when the means to suppress crime had not been so quick to be judgmental, officially scrutinized at the federal level, and often overruled internal policy and procedures.

Within the last few decades, because of the advancement of technology, chat sites, and excessive phone use, kids have grown up living in a world of weapons portrayed by Hollywood and video games—a phony world in which only the perceived bad guys lose. Or worse, the police are portrayed as the bad guys. Far too many have become acclimated and desensitized to the lethality and use of a weapon for retaliation and revenue to confront and pursue crime while armed with a weapon.

Patrol officers throughout the US are increasingly finding juveniles in possession of a firearm during contact more each year than in previous years. Casualties while patrolling the streets continue to mount; fewer and fewer young people are willing to wear a badge. Many who consider the career leave with early retirement seek work in the private sector or as security guards. Public opinion has moved in this "blame the officer" across the entire justice system.

Some major cities like New York, Los Angeles, and Chicago are witnessing urban war zones in residential neighborhoods. Gang and non-gang random shootings are reported each evening on the news. Lenient judges release criminals without bail; the guilty are happy to return to the crimes they were initially arrested for. Some involve serious felonies committed by men with extensive criminal histories. Liberal leaning politicians, district (county) attorneys, and some judges recommend leniency in sentencing. They recommend counseling for criminals rather than incarceration for someone awaiting trial.

Even in conservative states, this tendency is growing. Policing is becoming more like soldiering. Officers work on a restricted platform, like final centurions. Anyone who selects "justice" as a career goes out first to protect the public and guard the gates of the city, but in a restricted capacity, he or she is too often restrained to control crime or bring career criminals to prison. Why are so few Americans afraid to say, "This is costing us too much? We are no longer safe in our homes, our cars, or in public parks or buildings. We are fed up with living in fear of violence!"

Social anarchy has not yet hit an intolerable breaking point for enough citizens to demand a change in policy, but anarchy can happen if left unchecked. We do not expect military personnel to confront an evil-intentioned enemy in a combat zone as nothing but simple observers and bystanders. Military troops are trained to react to sudden violence with proactive steps to bring down the enemy; the same goes for policing. Truth be told, policing our streets is not an easy job; we should not be making that job more difficult.

Sometimes, it is not pretty.

Prioritizing a person's credentials of achievement based on higher education, ethnicity, and political affiliation as our guardians may be important in some circumstances, but less important than hiring and training the recruit with the right mental attitude, character, and willingness to serve others and the law. The majority of officers at every level, men and women from all backgrounds, will do the job if allowed. They do not retreat from adversity. Watch an episode of the reality show Reelz Police Live, or COPS, and you will see what these brave men and women are exposed to. Why would we want the police and corrections officers working in high-security prisons to function like white-collar workers or academics? Does an advanced degree make an officer more compassionate? More empathetic? More tolerable? More capable? More willing to stop crime in its tracks?

Hard as we try or think the lesson to be learned by persuasion and tolerance does not always work, a view of recent 'peace rally's' have shown otherwise.

The Ultimate Retaliation

Law enforcement personnel assigned to specialized units such as narcotics, fugitive apprehension, and gang units must be vigilant regarding this type of experienced career criminal. My personal experience and the testimony of others show offenders might attempt to identify the law enforcement personnel and staff assigned to these specialized units. Why? Because they know these are the people who will be scrutinizing them, interfering with their illegal activity, and sending them to prison. They will try to gain as much background information about you as we do about them. This information may be used to blackmail, intimidate, and compromise you and, worse yet, harm a family member.

In the extreme, some belonging to organized criminal groups and fanatical extremists will go so far as to place a "hit," an assassination, if they determine you are disrupting their criminal enterprises or organizations. They do their homework and have the means and resources to discover who you are. No one in policing, or even in the international intelligence espionage world, foresees this happening to them. Nor do they anticipate the full impact while pursuing an organized crime or subversive group can have on a community or even a nation. No one looks forward to hearing that they are targeted. It's so unnerving to be told you have become a hard target to hit. Or, as the convicts say, put "in the hat."

One of the best examples I recall was with Brian Parry. In, *Eye of the Devil,* author Brian describes in detail attempts by the notorious Los Angeles South Central street gang Eight Trey Crips to hit him, even to harm his family. At the time, Brian was a highly respected parole officer with the California Department of Corrections assigned to the Special Services Unit, SSU, in Los Angeles. The SSU is a hard-charging statewide unit assigned to apprehend the worst parole violators and prison gang members released to the streets--those who violated parole.

During the 1992 Los Angeles riots, the Eight Trey Crips were identified as major players. Brian, having prior dealings with Eight Trey, along with other parole agents and the Los Angeles Police Department, made the arrest of several members. I suggest you read his book to determine what efforts these groups will take when authorities confront them before they seek revenge. So, would it become my time?

MY PURPOSE

CHAPTER 4
THE PATH I TOOK

I did not perceive my future career path in those first years, as I had not given much thought to those I would eventually deal with—those repeat offenders displaying the nature, character, brazenness, and intricacies of a career criminal mindset. These types of offenders can be found in and are members of organizations such as prison gangs, crime syndicates, terror cells, cartels, and other local gang groups. For the most part, I still needed to fully perceive my career as part of a bigger picture of organized crime throughout the US and across the globe. I was learning the basics to earn respect from my peers.

Once confronted with such adversaries, our careers took on a new meaning. We discovered factions of a higher echelon within the murky, subversive criminal world—members of structured organizations with tentacles that reached far across state and national borders.

These organized criminal factions operated with their own set of rules. They were determined to achieve whatever corrupt or destructive activity they were pursuing, even while incarcerated. I realized that local officers working the streets did not have access to information to understand the complexity of the criminal operations they could or would encounter.

Local peace officers were not officers or agents in the know. Even veteran members of specialized units outside of their assignment and jurisdiction did not see how criminal tentacles reached across the country. This organized criminal threat was yet to be realized and included in professional training. A few of us did learn about it, but this career path was one that few chose. I was learning it takes time to get "the whole picture from the inside. For most of my career, I specialized in prison gangs, narcotics, and street gangs. In each of these assignments, I attempted to prioritize the intelligence collection process to identify the "who, what, where, how, and why" of a group, individual, or situation.

The Keys of Intelligence

Beginning in 1974, I attended law enforcement training courses on intelligence collection and analysis that

Graduation from Jump School 1966

emphasized the importance of applying the intelligence collection process to assist enforcement efforts. However, my informal initial exposure to understanding the application of working intelligence began in 1966 after completing Airborne (Jump) School. I was assigned to the Signal Company, 6th Special Forces Group at Fort Bragg, North Carolina. During my assignment with Special Forces stateside, I was exposed to many soldering skills, and I learned about the various communications equipment employed by Special Forces. When asked, I answered with respect, "I was assigned with the 6th Special Forces." I was in awe and somewhat intimidated by their company; they were older, wiser, and more mature, except for the few like me who were recently assigned. I'm sure my feelings were like those of a minor-league baseball player called into the major league for the first time.

Then, many of the company's noncommissioned officers (NCOs) had already served at least one tour in Vietnam. A few unmarried NCOs who chose to live on base were assigned as our barracks cadre. They had their room in our old wood coal-heated barracks, located on "Smoke Bomb Hill."

During work assignments, training, and evening hours, they would share their experiences with us. They talked about their experiences in Vietnam, the importance of Intelligence Collection, source development, and various Signal Intelligence usage. They also emphasized the importance of

Preparing to jump

caring for your equipment, perseverance, and other interesting subjects.

However, as a young, private first-class (PFC), I did not fully grasp the significance of this duty assignment. As time went on, I got it. Any influence or bravado from the street was gone. They were and are the real deal. The exposure I gained as a young man from these most highly dedicated, brave, and professional soldiers has had a lasting effect on me throughout my life. However, after more than a year on this assignment, I did not want the Vietnam War to pass me by, so I volunteered and put in a 1049 transfer to Vietnam. I will say that, at some point, I was able to renew acquaintances.

The Special Forces organizational structure shaped my thought process at the start of my law enforcement career. My military exposure helped me write proposals, and I learned to work with a team. Later, I used their organizational concepts as I proposed plans to create new gang associations, task forces, and functional operational principles. I seldom speak of specifics of my time in the military for personal reasons in keeping my own council. This is my choice. I am no hero or warrior, but I truly admire those who are and the many others who served, especially those who lost their lives and limbs. Only those familiar with the old-school military mentality and the earlier Vietnam era years would understand how things were accomplished and that had an impact on my life. Today, I remain a disabled veteran, deemed so by the Veterans Administration, certainly not of my own choosing.

The Foundation- Years in Cochise County

In 2016, I started reading long-forgotten yearly journals I had kept. Regrettably, I shredded them and gave away many photos and documents I had saved, now regarded as historical stuff. I now believe I did so out of the personal rejection and discontent I was experiencing.

Perhaps it was from a self-imposed rebuff, realizing I was no longer part of the club, in the car, as the convicts say. In other words, you are either in or out. As I tell this, I wish I had those photos and other mementos to jog my memory of the many changes my career included. At times, these changes came about unexpectedly as newer, broader opportunities arose, but there were a few disappointments, as I recall. Then again, I never considered that I would be describing important events and the lessons I learned over those years.

Let's begin in 1974, when I was employed with the Cochise County Sheriff's Office in a newly formed detective unit on the southeastern Arizona border with Mexico. The county seat is Bisbee, and the most populous city is Sierra Vista. The county borders southwestern New Mexico and the northwestern Mexican state of Sonora, so the border requires constant surveillance. I worked there for two years, up until 1976. Then I transferred to the newly created Arizona Drug Control District's (ADCD) Narcotics Strike Force in Cochise County. I was inspired to work near the area named for the Chiricahua Apache chief, a critical war leader during the Apache Wars, and the county's rich southwestern history. At the time, I was reading historical accounts in the southwest, of which Cochise County was a major centerpiece.

For someone who grew up in Los Angeles County, California, working in this rural environment taught me life-changing lessons. Unlike what I knew from observing the mighty Los Angeles Police and Sheriff's Departments in action with all their resources, specialty units, and assignments, it was a challenge out there along the Mexican border. We were on our own in a vast landscape of desert and sagebrush, a wide open land interspersed with mesquite trees, separated by miles between a city and a township. We carried our own resources in our undercover vehicles. We created our own initiative and ingenuity; we innovated and acted independently to arrest the bad guys.

Throughout those years in Cochise County, I worked alongside many dedicated law enforcement officers. I learned how these rural officers handled encounters with different criminals and how they anticipated crimes. I was a reliable team player on a good team.

However, even though I had great experiences and increased knowledge on how to suppress crime, I felt I had not hit my prime. My years in Cochise County with the Sheriff's Office and the Strike Force were formative: making my bones and laying the foundation for the rest of my career. Forming the Detective Unit was a new concept to professionalize the Sheriff's Office that intrigued me. Until then, the sheriff used mostly patrol deputies to investigate crimes without a formal, plain-clothed unit.

Lt to Rt Frank Gonzales, me, Dave Fox, Richie Martinez

The Detective Unit was administered by a tough Lieutenant, Doug Knipp, and supervised by the youngest of the bunch, Sergeant Ritchie Martinez. Ritchie had been assigned to one of Arizona's original metro narcotics enforcement units, which was deactivated before my time with the Sheriff's Office. Ritchie was intelligent, energetic, and one of the first officers to attend the intelligence collection and analysis training held by the California Department of Justice. Detectives Frank Gonzales, Dave Fox, and I were unit members. Dave and Frank had a nose for sniffing out narcotics cases, keeping us busy and spirited. All of us except Ritchie were veterans; we did not let him forget "that we had served." Both Dave and Ritchie remain close friends.

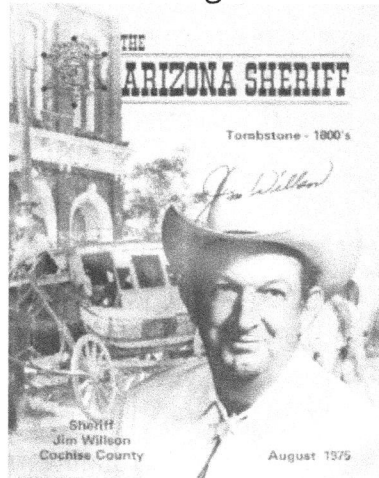

THE
ARIZONA SHERIFF

Tombstone - 1800's

Jim Willson

Sheriff
Jim Willson
Cochise County

August 1975

Though few in numbers, we were effective as we roamed the county, attending to felony investigations. Because we understood the importance of the intelligence collection process and source development, our specialty became narcotics. Even though our time there is lost in memory, we were highly effective and creative, working with few restrictions. It was indeed a time of lessons learned for all of us. We could not have been so successful if our unit had suffered from administrative restraints. But most important to us was the support and encouragement from one of the greatest sheriffs in Arizona history, Sheriff Jimmy Willson. A legit Arizona cowboy who spoke Spanish, Jimmy could tell a story with the best of them. After Sheriff Willson's term expired in 1976, Undersheriff Jimmy Judd became Sheriff. He, too, was supportive of drug enforcement efforts. Sheriff Willson then joined the Narcotics Strike Force as a liaison spokesperson.

I recall, on one occasion, around 1975, a group of Arizona legislators came to Bisbee, Arizona, ostensibly for a meeting of both Republicans and Democrats. Sheriff Jimmy Willson took them across the Arizona border to Naco, Sonora, Mexico, to recreate. At that time, it was before the Mexican cartels had a foothold along the Arizona border and "gringos" were welcomed—an era when politicians spoke civilly to one another and could get things done across party lines. Love and respect were mutual for both sheriffs.

The Detective Unit worked several cases with the DEA, Customs, ATF, and Border Patrol. They were seasoned, dedicated federal government professionals with access to information from Mexico that bordered Arizona. I recall working with Agents Hector Berrellez, Tommy Gomez, Charlie Lugo, Ernie Lowe, Fred Ball, and Hank Murray with ATF. In addition, I learned what a professional was like from listening to and observing one of my earliest mentors with US Customs, Special Agent Jim Smith. We in the detective unit were eager, thriving in our own right, and still learning our craft.

While still with the Cochise County Sheriff's Office, something significant happened. I wrote a letter and skeletal outline of a Narcotics Task Force concept to the Arizona Attorney General, Bruce Babbitt. I read in the newspaper he was considering a plan to stem the drug flow from Mexico. I listed my experiences working on drug cases along the Mexican border and enclosed my vision. I still have those documents.

I explained what was necessary logistically to meet

his goal: specialized surveillance equipment and intelligence collection. My proposal worked its way back to the Sheriff, who called me into his office. I thought I was in deep trouble. However, Sheriff Willson was pleased, probably surprised, and said we were invited to a meeting in Tucson with state officials to discuss implementing a Strike Force concept. If someone were to do something as brazen as that today, break the chain of command, they would be fired or severely disciplined. But then again, I worked for Sheriff Willson. He understood that good ideas most often arise from the lower ranks, employees working the front lines of any occupation.

In 1978, I transferred to Tucson with the ADCD Narcotics Strike Force. Tucson, located in Pima County, was then, as now, a prime trans-shipment point for the storage and distribution of drugs coming from Mexico.

The Intelligence Process Comes to Arizona

Our focus was to reduce the number of drugs within the four counties that border Mexico. It emphasized enforcement and the intelligence process. Simultaneously, the same emphasis on the intelligence process was addressed by the Arizona Department of Public Safety (AZDPS). Two legislative state-funded agencies were charged with this same mandate and funded by law.

As the years progressed, a great deal of rivalry existed between the two agencies at the administrative level. There was great competition regarding which agency should be responsible for this function. However, Captain Frank Root's leadership and expertise kept the organization functioning at the officer level (AZ DPS, Intelligence Division Captain Frank Root), author of *Law Enforcement Intelligence: Critical Elements*. Frank had expertise in the intelligence process using automated data systems in Arizona, way ahead of his time. He has remained my friend, and I have always valued his expertise in the intelligence arena.

Much can be said about how the ADCD came about. But without a doubt, Pima County Attorney Terry Grimble was its driving force; the intelligence-driven concept was innovative. Its primary service was to assist other law enforcement agencies in counties that border Mexico to fight those carrying drugs into the US.

The ADCD first-line supervision, field agents, clerical staff, and the analysts were all dedicated professionals; we felt we were working towards a cause greater than ADCD. But as with many great ideas, the need to expand beyond our initial niche became costly and problematic. As time passed, much scrutiny with accusations of financial loss was leveled against the agency; close interpersonal relations between a changing administration and many personnel with the ADCD team became confused and distant. Nepotism among new hires and changing administrators, too many with little or no experience in law enforcement as applied to the intelligence process, eroded our esprit de core. During these times of uncertainty and confusion, one bright light could always be dependent upon: Supervisor Frank Teachout, a great leader and cop. Frank deserves full recognition.

My time with the ADCD was mixed with extreme highs of working narcotic conspiracy cases, organized crime, and undercover assignments. I am especially proud of my time on loan with the Tucson Metro Narcotics, Tucson Police Department (under the leadership of Lieutenant Orville "Andy" Ridgely and Sergeants Glean Hendricks, and Werner Wolfe). But in the end, it was bittersweet. While with the ADCD, I still felt I had not achieved my full potential. Again, I was a team player on many different teams; together, we learned valuable lessons, but my perseverance was wearying.

The Reckoning in My Journey

In 1982, I took an assignment in Lake Havasu, Arizona, mainly to escape what was happening at the ADCD headquarters in Tucson. During that time, various groups within state politics, real estate, and investors were exploring the possibilities of bringing legalized gambling to Arizona to compete with Nevada.

My time in Lake Havasu, however, was short-lived. I took the assignment with the belief that my purpose was to look into and sort out who the deep-pocketed investors looking to buy beach property along the Colorado River. We were trying to determine who had ties to organized crime elements out of Las Vegas, Nevada or elsewhere. I was to approach this assignment low-key and, at the same time, assist other agencies in drug investigations.

Two significant events happened. I quickly learned that the territory from Parker to Bullhead City, Arizona, was steeped in political infighting, rumors, and innuendos of corruption. This problem was exacerbated by scrutiny from an ADCD management team in Tucson headquarters whose perception of me was greatly maligned and misconceived.

Undercover in Yuma County Jail

They did not understand my circumstances as the finder and keeper of sensitive information. I was uncovering shady characters, political influence, criminal investors, and criminal associations along the Colorado River. I met a valued source, newspaper reporter Tom Riley, an Irish transplant from Boston who became a confidant and good friend until his death.

Tom, a dogged, determined reporter, passed his findings to me, along with those of other citizen sources who kept an eye on criminal, financial, and political influences. However, I had to convey these findings verbally and provide research through written intelligence reports back to Tucson, for which I seldom if ever received feedback. To my memory, the only person who took an interest in my findings was AZ DPS Detective Tom Davis. Supposedly, they were viewed as rival agencies at that time. A few other conflicts arose, for which I voiced dissatisfaction. The new ADCD Tucson administration ordered an alternative mandate that put my professional career in potential jeopardy, leading me to hire an attorney and depose those accusers. There is much to add to the story, but now, with my legal counsel, they have ceased harassment. Those administrators were aware I had much to say to a state merit system council if requested. They decided not to take it that far.

Before I left Lake Havasu, a second significant event altered me personally. I had a spiritual awakening, a life change in character and attitude; this resulted in a clearer understanding of what was important in life's journal. The ADCD placeholder administration said to my friends, "Paco has changed." They were right. But not because of their perception and the actions they took against me. Had those administrators cared to take time to ask why I changed my outlook on life instead of relying on their false perception, I could have led them to Pastor/Evangelist Larry Reed, a former heroin addict and resident of San Quentin prison in California.

I spotted a simple small flier on the driver's side windshield, maybe 5x8" or maybe the size of a "Wanted" poster, after leaving the police station. It had a simple message with a photograph that to me looked like someone who had been "around". It related the story of a former heroin addict and San Quentin graduate and how he changed his life. After reading it, I casually left it on my front passenger seat and took no further notice. A week later, as I pulled into my home driveway, I happened to glance over and I picked it up. He was scheduled to speak at a storefront in a run-down shopping center that day. After dinner, I told my wife I was going to see what this "public speaker" was all about. Little did I know that my naïveté was drawing me to a message of redemption. From that day forward, my life has changed. I still have rough edges that show up now and then, and I do enjoy Maker's Mark® bourbon on occasion. I guess you could say I'm still a work in progress; but aren't we all.

A more in-depth summary of what was transpiring within the ADCD is explained by Neil Tietjen, former ADCD Tucson field operations supervisor, in his book, *Old School Narc*. Neil related what he personally endured under this new management team—hired for the politically expedient purpose of curtailing the agency's existence. Though Neil's situation and circumstances differed from mine, the same political and internal administrative techniques were used against both of us.

I spoke with Neil briefly a week before he went into the hospital to get his approval to reference him and his book, and we talked about many things from the past. Sadly, this strong, robust man succumbed to his battle with cancer in the time I was writing this book.

The Awakening of My Journey

By late 1983, the Arizona legislature was in the process of dismantling the ADCD Narcotics Strike Force. As a result, most field agents could transfer to the AZ DPS Criminal Investigation Division. For me, this opportunity was like finding the Ark of the Covenant or Blackbeard's Treasure. It was a turning point in my career. I moved my family to Phoenix and joined the AZ DPS. I was assigned to the Intelligence Division. Shortly after, a slot opened up, which allowed me to work with prison gangs. I quickly volunteered. While working in Cochise County and Tucson, I knew there were gangs in the prison system that grouped themselves according to race.

Over the years, I have worked on investigations and participated in the arrests and investigations of several ex-convicts. A few were rumored to have ties with these prison gangs. Most officers thought it was just a prison problem. Little did we all realize how misplaced that thinking was. What I learned became the lessons I now share about criminals who make crime a way of life, even from behind prison walls.

CHAPTER 5
LESSONS FROM PRISON GANGS

Prior to my prison gang assignment, I was left with some big shoes to fill. Since the late 1970s DPS had criminal investigators working in liaison with AZ DOC prison investigators. Three of those predecessors were Bobby Griffith, Mark Brown, and Bobby Halliday (who, years later, became the DPS Director). Eventually, each was promoted to Sergeant or moved on to other assignments. I was next in line.

From around 1975 to my assignment induction, several murders in prison and on the streets were attributed to prison infighting. The Department of Public, Criminal Investigations Division had investigators who routinely responded to these incidents. Leading up to 1983, several significant events involving prison gang members caught the attention of both the prison and law-enforcement authorities. They recorded an upswing of murders and assaults by Hispanic inmates. Also, critical information obtained by prison authorities led to the Florence prison maximum security complex, CB-6. A search displayed detonating cords, blasting caps, and other contraband in the possession of suspected Aryan Brotherhood members. Corrections investigators collected these items from inmate cells. Intelligence collected and from source information indicated that a few of these members had ties with the highly visible nationwide white extremist movement at that time.

Thus, I began this assignment knowing full well that there was much work ahead and many things to learn. Assaults and murders of rival Hispanic factions in the prison system continued to grow. Phoenix was feeling a spinoff from an unfolding storm involving various criminal street and prison groups in Los Angeles. Retired Phoenix Police Department Detective Alex Fermina, an early member of the gang squad, said they had received information from the South Mountain precinct saying the Los Angeles-based Crip gangsters were active in Phoenix. At the time, the squad did not realize that a serious problem existed—one connected to seriously schooled street gang members.

The distribution of crack cocaine led some entrepreneurs from various Los Angeles black gangs, mostly Crips, into the Phoenix market, perhaps thinking this market would be easy to control. During this period, black gang sets had existed for a few years in LA, and they were responsible for numerous shootings. They came to Phoenix thinking this same swagger would hold court in Arizona. However, in the aftermath, they ran out. After numerous arrests and convictions of their gang members, a substantial number were housed in the Arizona prison system at Florence. Those housed in Arizona's jurisdiction formed a group called the United Crip Gang. They made my life and the AZ DOC Florence prison working with the Special Security Unit led by Sergeant Able Garza very busy for a while.

Detective Fermina recalled an event involving these gangs in Phoenix. This specific event led to increased resources being dedicated to Phoenix police gang squads. A Phoenix Fire Department truck responding to a fire at 21st St. and Broadway took gun fire from suspect gang members. Additionally, from 1984 through the 1990s, the Los Angeles gang phenomenon gained notoriety in the area. Street gang turf fights and rivalries escalated into several shootings throughout Maricopa County, even in non-traditional neighborhoods. Car thefts increased as gang members needed merchandise to sell for drugs; drug distribution at high schools, in malls, and even in public parks increased.

Things were heating up in Arizona, and I don't mean the weather. By 1985, this growing street gang concern as well as events occurring within the prison system, led to the first federally funded Prison Gang Task Force in Arizona.

The Arizona Prison Gang Task Force

Arizona had suffered serious crime waves throughout the mid-to-late 1970s. The state needed this task force. In 1985, the Arizona Prison Gang Task Force was created by a federal grant. Agency administrators handpicked the personnel for this stand-alone team. It consisted of supervisors, detectives, and investigators from the Department of Public Safety (DPS), the Arizona Department of Corrections (ADOC), the Attorney General's AG, investigators, and two full-time attorneys from the AG's office. Many readers who lived in Arizona may not have known of its existence. Even today.

First, there were repeated incidents of violent assaults and murders occurring within the Arizona prison system and across communities. ADOC noticed a steep escalation of violence after corrections officials became aware of prison gangs tied to California's prison gang problem.

Members represented several ethnic groups and races. Vicious murder resulted from the internal purging of rivalries between gangs within the prison system. Arizona was also experiencing tremendous population growth and a noticeable increase in violence, aggravated assaults, armed robberies, and drug rip-offs, particularly in the Phoenix metropolitan area and in Tucson, Resulting in the expansion of new prisons throughout Arizona. Analysts from DPS saw a pattern: much of this criminal activity traced back to released prison inmates. The ADOC identified several suspects of these crimes—they all had an affiliation with a prison gang.

News outlets began extensive investigative reporting that became everyday TV videos, alarming stories people did not want to see at the evening dinner hour. A citizen's outcry over this notoriety pressured the Arizona legislature, so Senators requested Attorney General Bob Corbin create new prosecution and enforcement measures under the office of the state Attorney General.

Specifically, the goal of the Arizona Prison Gang Task Force was to target the prison gang problem operationally. Its primary mission was twofold: to glean intelligence and sources from within the prisons and target released prison gang members who were committing street crimes. The goal was also to add gang enhancement charges along with formal charges to significantly enhance sentencing. Primarily, prosecutors had to prove the offender was a gang member. AG Attorneys Steve LaMar and Rhonda Davis met the challenge and overcame fierce opposition from the defendants' attorneys. Out of necessity, I wrote a template using seven criteria to substantiate data that proved gang membership. This tool was adopted and used in court proceedings successfully. The Gang Member Identifying Criteria was later adopted into Arizona Criminal Statutes.

Since my assignment with DPS was in prison gangs, I was tasked with working intelligence and concentrating on source development and offender target selection of those members once they returned to the street. My routine was to spend two or three days each week at one of the prisons or jail. My liaison partner, Investigator Joe Savalas, from ADOC, was also assigned to assist with the Task Force. He worked at the Central Unit, a maximum-security correctional facility in Florence, Arizona. At that time, this facility housed most inmates previously identified as members of prison gangs.

When assigned to a specialized unit like gangs, narcotics, fugitive, and robbery, you become familiar with the same names—they keep coming up. The information came from other agencies working with the same people, from confidential sources, from private citizens, and from off-hand informants. I always checked for the most recent photograph—a driver's license or prison/jail mugshot photos—to see who we were dealing with; sometimes, looks can be deceiving.

As time went on, I got to recognize some of these subjects' personality traits and unique crime methods. I could sometimes reason about who had committed the crime from a distance, hearing about it. It helped to know who was released from prison and out on the streets. But getting to know a person in his element up close, in the environment, amongst his peers is much different from looking at a photograph or rap sheet. Prisons and jails provide unique views to those who know how to look and listen for personality traits and character flaws. These come to life in an interview, for good and for bad. I observed how an inmate responded to situations and his interpersonal relationships with authority figures and peers.

Because of my familiarity with many of the prison gang members before the prison gang unit's existence, I could provide some "good to know information." We used intelligence collection and source development to make targeted arrests. We conducted search warrants and apprehended parole violators. We concentrated on drug dealers and close associates of the AB because they were the most active on the streets and filled most of the unit's

The Arizona Mexican Mafia

arrests. However, some investigative team members were unfamiliar with *released inmates*, primarily those *still in prison*, unless they had contact with them before incarceration. The AZ NMM became most active in prison and on the streets soon after the prison gang task force ended. Today they are known as The Arizona Mexican Mafia.

As we worked cases, a couple of unit members wanted to go with me to the oldest prison in Florence, Arizona, called the Central Complex. This prison still had the appearance and feel of the old-style prisons, much like San Quentin and Old Folsom in California. The Central Unit Complex was encased with high concrete mortar walls. The old-style gun towers were visible from a long distance before reaching the prison, and many cells operated manually by keys still had this mystique. But eventually the Florence surrounding area was expanded and remodeled, with two Special Management Units 1 & 2 and medium custody facilities. I will never forget the first time I stepped into the two legendary California prisons. It made me humble to consider the stories I had read and heard while attending the CPGTF meetings.

On this visit, my peer task force officers wanted a first-hand look at how things "go down in prison." There is an unspoken universal rule: cops don't hang around prisons. The thought, most generally, is that once an arrest is made and a sentence is rendered, the cop's work is over; the rest is left to corrections personnel.

On the day we took the tour, we entered the South Unit, a medium-custody-level section next to the Central Prison. We knew there were several members of the AB and the NMM housed there. It was at a time before we started validating inmates as gang members and placing them in security housing, so many were still in medium custody prison units. My peers were Joe Savalas from the prison, Detective Mike "MJ" Mauser, and Dave Pratt from DPS, all physically capable officers who could handle unforeseen situations. We weren't the "Wild Bunch," but we exuded confidence; we were assertive, proactive, not easily intimidated, and we were up for any challenge.

The inmates in the South Unit lived in open bay Army Quonset huts, not prison cell blocks. The complex had a large open recreational yard with a baseball field, a handball court, and a weight pile (workout area). Within the prison, the yard had a Snack Shack. The Snack Shack was a service the prison industry provided but one the inmates managed. It sold candy, soda, and snacks. Inmates paid with tokens deducted from their accounts. In reality, it was controlled by the Aryan Brotherhood. The AB was suspected of using the Snack Shack to sneak drugs into the prison through a private outside vendor who supplied goods. However, we were never able to prove it.

This part of the story requires some visualization. To reach the South Unit, we entered from the Central Complex, the main sally port, and walked to the South Unit. There were two gates into the South Unit. One was the preferred way, which was closed to the unit's glassed-in guard post operated by uniformed staff. It had a view of the prison yard and the Snack Shack. The second entrance was through a gate about a hundred yards down the far north end of the athletic field along a sidewalk leading to the first gate where the officer's guard post was located. We chose to go through the more isolated north gate, hoping we could approach the Snack Shack unnoticed.

We wanted to catch the inmates by surprise. As we approached the Snack Shack, we were confronted by all the ABs in the South Unit and their associates. They had seen us coming through the gate, so they confronted us. One AB stepped out in front, acting as the group's spokesperson, and laid a heavy dose of scandalous messages laced with "MF'ers" on us. Mike "MJ" Mauser stepped out on our side to confront him. Other inmates were also loud and agitated, telling us we didn't belong in the prison, much less in their yard. There were many more of them than there were of us.

Of course, we responded by telling them our badge gave us the authority to go anywhere in the state; we also verbalized our own profane message. It got really tense quickly, and neither side planned to back down. I can't say we were chest-to-chest, but it was getting there. Finally, after what seemed like forever, the AB group broke up, and we went on our way. It was one of those moments when we officers looked at one another and said, "THAT WAS INTERESTING!"

So, why did we put ourselves in this position? Our intention was not to provoke a confrontation, nor did we expect such a quick reaction. No doubt we underestimated the animosity towards the APGTF. Should we have known better? This was an important lesson for my visiting peers. The event was an example of how things can go down in a prison really quickly based on inmates' group thinking. Such direct, aggressive action also occurs once these inmates are released onto city streets. This is one of the important lessons I shared at law enforcement conferences. Officers must always be ready to expect the unexpected in any situation involving ex-prisoners. It also confirmed everything I had been telling my peers with the APGTF about my experiences with inmates I had encountered.

Thanks to my partner, Joe Savalas, this was not the first time hostile inmates had confronted me. Another similar incident occurred when I went to the prison before the AB incident. Joe and I wanted to see what was happening in the east prison unit yard next to the central prison complex. Joe was no stranger to the inmate population. He had previously worked on the prison search team. We entered the prison yard and approached a bunch of black inmates sitting on a table. Joe called out to them loudly and referred to them as Crips.

They were not. They were older Mau-Mau members of a black inmate prison gang who did not like the style of all the Crips coming into the prison system. To them, what Joe said was disrespectful. These men immediately jumped off the table and came at us. They were very angry. Swearing and yelling, they surrounded us. One of them got right up into Joe's face, and I had to pull him back before it came to blows. Again, the staff quickly responded, which may have prevented a serious disturbance. The deputy warden subsequently banned Joe from the unit. I hadn't seen or heard from Joe for many years until I contacted him, advising him that I would use his name in my book. I reminded Joe of these incidents when we worked together. Joe laughed. He did not scare easily.

Was there a bit of bravado from us in the prison yard? Probably, but it's necessary to show adversaries who they're going up against, especially when they consider themselves invincible. I do not advocate, however, that justice officers use such boldness without a specific purpose in mind. That day in Florence prison, we needed to show those aggressive inmates that there is a specialized law enforcement group willing to go into prisons and put their criminal activities in check.

By the time the APGTF was operational, prison gangs were well-established in Arizona. They had been entrenched in the Florence prison complex for over a decade and had spread to other prison facilities. To catch up to their threats, we had to use unique operational and intelligence collection methods.

The Telephone Plot

The Prison Gang Task Force was established for the purpose of controlling the AB and two Mexican prison factions vying for power. For some time, my partner Joe Savalas and I wanted to interview a high-echelon AB shot caller. It was well known that he had a lengthy

criminal history and a reputation for an extreme dislike of authority; even in prison, he was defiant to the core. Joe was familiar with him; I was not, except for his reputation. We also felt he would refuse to come out of the lockdown cell if he knew he was to be interviewed. He had refused interviews with other officials, and even if he did come, he would likely tell us to "fuck off." Yet we were determined to

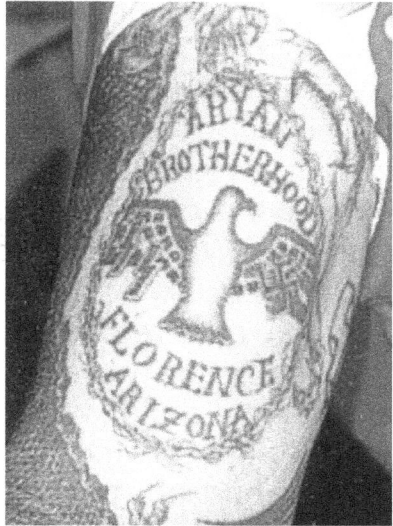

interview this guy. Perhaps a bit of ego was involved when we came up with the "Telephone Plot." Here's how it worked:

The inmate was housed in the lockdown security facility within the prison—in a cell block separated from other inmate housing units and from the medical/administration building. Inmates never left the housing facility except to go to a medical appointment, to attend court, or for other authorized circumstances. When leaving the facility, an inmate wore leg irons and handcuff restraints and was escorted by two officers. The Deputy Warden of Security Housing told us that this inmate was receiving treatment at medical for an injury, and he would not refuse transport if he believed he was going in for treatment.

This visit required a very short vehicle ride to the medical office unit, located in the same building as the Investigation and Inspection Office (I & I). Conveniently, this was near Joe's office. When entering the investigation office, a secretary verified that visitors had official business. She greeted everyone entering the building where Joe's basement office sat. Access to his office required walking down a narrow staircase, about half a dozen steps and his office door faced the staircase. We planned to have the inmate escorted under the ruse of going to a medical appointment. This plan required the escort officers to help as part of the plot; timing was everything. We also needed cooperation and timing with the secretary; this took more than a bit of convincing.

Our part of the scenario began when the inmate was brought to the investigator's office instead of to the medical area. The inmate was told someone wanted to speak with him about a pending appeal he had filed before the courts. As soon as the inmate and escort arrived, the secretary had them wait at her location. She called us from another office to let us know the inmate was coming down the stairs with the officers. That call gave us enough time to set up. The escorting officers kept him standing at the top of the stairs before entering the basement office. He was still restrained in handcuffs and leg irons. I was standing in front of a desk in Joe's office.

My back was to the inmate. I stood in front of the desk, pretending to speak to someone on the phone. A small chair sat in front of the desk for the inmate. When I heard them descend the stairs, I began yelling, cussing, demanding , and giving orders to my pretend telephone person. It had to come across as if I were someone with authority and audacity, someone who could make things happen. I spoke loudly so the inmate could hear. I continued this charade while he stood there, waiting. It felt like a lifetime had passed, but, in reality, it probably took no more than several seconds. Then I slammed the phone down, wheeled around, and said as sternly as I could, "Are you ____? I am Paco from DPS. Sit down. I want to talk to you."

Standing just a couple of feet from me, the inmate looked surprised. The ruse caught him off guard and perhaps left him outside his comfort zone. The inmate, in total compliance, sat down in the chair, and we asked the officer to remove the restraints before they stepped out. We always had a pack of cigarettes to offer to the inmate if they chose to smoke. Though this practice is not used or greatly frowned upon today, it seemed to put them somewhat at ease. He was guarded, respectful, and confident; not arrogant as expected. We spent some time with him—enough time to recognize how he held status among his fellow Aryan Brotherhood members. In the end, he said, "I was wondering when you were going to pull me out." He was not a source and did not give up inside information; it was a "get-to-know-you" interview. Perhaps he was as curious to know who we were as we were with him. You can assume, but you never really know what others are thinking under duress.

Joe and I devised the "telephone" plot technique as we were willing to do whatever it took to collect needed information in an interview. To accomplish our mission, we had to be creative, knowing that with some of these bad guys, we had only one shot. What we gleaned from the telephone plot proved invaluable in assessing the characteristics of those who hold influence within a prison gang. The interview would never have occurred had we not thought outside the box. This surprising technique proved that regardless of an inmate's status, reputation, or criminal history, a clever interview technique can break through their defenses.

In later years, when I spoke at conferences, I mentioned the telephone plot on a few occasions. I have since wondered if anyone has tried it. I also consider such innovations a lesson in measuring the detective's strengths and weaknesses. Not everyone can verbally go toe-to-toe with a hardcore career criminal convict who exhibits an anti-authority attitude. Many people are so concerned about being disrespected, put-down, and intimidated by such a conflict that they dare not take the risk of responding in a way they would later regret.

The interviewer should already know these inmates can verbally out-jab you if you are not prepared. They are familiar with verbal judo, putting down each other with intimidation as a defense mechanism, or calling out a bluff during a confrontation. I learned this lesson the hard way one day while working for the MCSO Jail Intelligence Unit at the old Madison jail. During a verbal exchange in front of a cellblock with a particular AB inmate, a dangerous cop hater unleashed a barrage of profane and challenging insults on me for all of his fellow cellmates to hear. In my response, I recovered somewhat but felt he got the best of me in the exchange. I never should have tried to reason with someone who exhibited such animosities in that kind of environment. Lesson learned: always expect the unexpected.

Pulling off this "telephone plot" even stretched our comfort zone. When working with a partner, make sure you are both in tune with the same message, work with no egos, and do not try to outdo each other. Total cooperation allows the two to speak as one.

This was my experience with my second investigative partner at the prison. Investigator Ken Lucas was stationed at the ADOC Florence Complex. Ken was eventually assigned to the Security Threat Group Unit (STGU), where he worked for me. Over the years, Ken and I conducted many interviews together, and we had chemistry. It was uncanny when I was trying to find an inmate's answer. Ken would resolve the issue as if he had read my mind. We complimented one another's style and never stooped to compete.

I will now reveal a secret only Ken and I knew until now. At every opportunity during our interviews, we would tell the inmates how the Lord could change their circumstances. I don't recall any inmates who took offense, but I'm sure they were surprised. Sometimes, the perception we portrayed reached an emotion the inmates had hidden. We kept these opportunities to ourselves, on the down low, as we knew that if the prison administration heard we were mentioning spiritual matters, they would question our logic. Score one for the right team. Ken later became one of Arizona's leading experts on prison gangs; he remains a precious brother. I am sure there is someone today who took our message to heart.

DPS Gang Squad-Top row left to right, Charlie Ruiz, Sgt. Steve Trethewy, Lt, Ray Lambertson, me. Bottom row left to right-Dave Sanchez, Ed Stock, Miguel Renteria.

The AZ DPS Gang Squad
When the grant for the APGTF expired around 1987, all members were assigned to different functions. I went back to the DPS Intelligence Division. A new gang squad was created and supervised by my good friend, Sergeant Steve Trethewy, whose expertise was with motorcycle gangs. Each squad member had a specialty, like street, prison, or motorcycle gangs. Although we were only one squad, we adopted a "force multiplier" concept perfected by the US Army Special Forces.

We worked together as a squad when the occasion called for full squad participation; at other times, we were free to work on our specialty. As an example, if the Mesa Police Department was having a street gang problem in a particular neighborhood, we would work together to address the issue. As a state agency, DPS had the authority to work statewide to assist Mesa P.D. This doubled the manpower and resources.

Another example of the squad's involvement where we provided intelligence and enforcement was with the annual motorcycle prison run to Florence, Arizona. I participated in this run for years. Sergeant Trethewy was in his element, always wanting to get ahead of the pack of motorcycles and pull them over. Although all motorcycle enthusiasts could participate in the prison run, it was spearheaded by "the one-percenters," The Dirty Dozen Motorcycle Club. This intense lawless biker club was later absorbed by the Hells Angels. The Angels now lead the pack during the run and have chapters in Arizona.

This event mandated full squad participation and called for additional resources from the DPS Highway Patrol Division and other law enforcement agencies. The gang squad, though small in number, recognized the benefits and rewards of assisting other law enforcement agencies.

Outside of those special circumstances, I continued to monitor prison gangs. I teamed up for a short stint with Detective John Allen assigned to the DEA Task Force, an intelligent, witty, and enthusiastic deputy with the Maricopa County Sheriff's Office (MCSO). He was working narcotics, so he wanted to learn more about the Aryan Brotherhood. John was handling a few confidential informants, and the name of an AB member with whom I was familiar kept coming up. Sources told John this particular individual was strung out on methamphetamine; he was threatening others, and the meth-user community was scared. I also heard rumors and knew that person had an outstanding arrest warrant. The target had been out of prison for about a year, but he was a danger to society as he had continued running and gunning. Though I had never spoken to him while he was in prison, I had observed him in the prison yard, so I knew his reputation. He was one of the biggest, most buffed-out white inmates I had observed in the prison system.

One day, John informed me that one of his confidential informants had made a controlled narcotics purchase from a residence, and he told John that AB member was going to be at this residence. John got a probable cause search warrant for the seller and house; he asked if I would like to come along. We were hoping the suspect would be there. We set up surveillance for a while and saw some people enter the residence, but not our guy. We were not sure if he was in the residence, a known methamphetamine user's house. The Sheriff's Office SWAT team made the entry. They flashed-banged the house upon entry, causing disorientation, and brought out to the backyard numerous handcuffed subjects. They lined them up in a sitting position against a brick wall in the backyard. There was little light, so we used flashlights to make identification.

Some officers were searching for the residence, and a couple of us were in the back trying to identify those taken from the house. As I walked along the row of subjects, I shined my light on each one. I had just reached the end of the line when I heard "pstt, pstt: (like someone was trying to get someone's attention), followed by "Paco, is that you? This is_____." I went over to the subject I had just walked past and shined my light on him. I was in disbelief. It was the AB member. His face was drawn in and hollow. He had lost so much weight that I did not recognize him. He said something to the effect of, "I got to talk to you, man; it's important!" He said this in front of others; this was not a good situation, and I knew instantly that he wanted to make a deal. He was so sure of himself, so used to intimidating others, and so strung out on meth that he didn't care what others thought. He didn't even care for his own safety.

A couple of months later, we arrested him again. One night, while surveilling him, we attempted to do a traffic stop, so we "lit him up." We ended up in a short pursuit through a residential neighborhood. We saw him trying to reach under his seat, and in doing so, he crashed his vehicle. He was a bit disoriented from the crash, so my partner, DPS Detective Bill Whitlow, dragged him out through the driver's side door window. We found a .9 mm pistol on the driver's side floor, so we booked him for felony possession of a firearm and for an outstanding warrant. He acted like he had a death row conviction with nothing else to lose.

Ultimately, he ended up being a real problem for me—including a flare-up and misunderstanding with another police agency in another investigation, which led to Intelligence Division Captain Mike Denney's intervention. The AB was so self-assured that attempts to fight a return to prison put me in a very awkward, precarious position. His defense attorney called me as a witness in one of his trials, and I did not want to reveal what I knew about him and my prior dealings with him. I learned that some criminals are so hell-bound that nothing can be done to deter them.

As I write the finishing touches to this journey, I'm sad to report that my partner that night, retired DPS Detective Bill Whitlow, lost his battle with cancer. In September 2023, retired DPS Detective Mike "MJ" Mauser and I, upon learning of Bill's condition, took a trip to Heber, Arizona, to visit with him. Though weak physically, he was strong spiritually and showed his old, very funny sense of humor.

I asked Bill if he remembered the night he pulled the AB out of the driver's side door window. He said with laughter, "Hey Paco, but you never told me he was one of the biggest and baddest Aryan Brother-hood members"!

The Obstructionist Effect

However, there were boogeymen in the works, so we need to get the structural barriers out in the open. Far too frequently, those authorities who keep their hands on the field of law enforcement prevent rapid change. Addressing changes in traditions with different agencies was challenging since they too faced opposition imposed by careerists in each organization. My challenge during the time of this incident was convincing certain prison officials of what I had learned from the CDCR by policy and procedures to address prison gangs—that the potential control of prison gangs could hold over facilities, staff, and fellow inmates. The influential career criminals and organized gangs behind bars understand the game authorities play; he creates a countermeasure for every new measure the justice team launches to maintain order. This I felt certain of.

The most frustrating thing for me was obstructionism from a handful of individuals holding positions of authority within the hierarchy of different departments I worked with, even some I worked for. Of course, in a broader perspective, there are career justice personnel in corrections, police, sheriffs, and even federal government officials who tried their best to improve controls. These criminal justice professionals did offer practical policies, but most required legislative support, which required additional tax dollars. Consequently, their ideas came up against the boogeymen within state and local agencies, career justice administrators who commanded top management jobs in their quest for self-glorification and promotion.

As a result, administrators and managers feel threatened by tax-dependent policy changes. It is easy for a career manager in any field to remain risk-averse to fresh initiatives and ideas from subordinates. Administrators become territorial about their areas of control. This resistance to accept suggestions from the lower ranks of personnel and civic committees is a people problem.

But this problem defines the structural resistance at all levels of government, all levels of justice institutions, and even private entities (including taxpayers who vote for justice administrators). Most recently, the problem of initiating positive change within criminal justice institutions has come to the attention of civic and legislative oversight committees established to analyze problems and offer legislators solutions. Who do these civic committee members go to for advice— the seated, senior administrator within these agencies who survives by political protection and maintaining the status quo? Those who do speak out today to identify malpractice and wrongdoing are labeled "whistleblowers" and will pay a price.

This issue is too important to gloss over. The inability of first-to-mid-level personnel to affect change, even when a problem is obvious in an environment where malfeasance and harm occurs, has an impact; it definitely impacted me at the time, but it still does. Our lack of ability to make practical changes based on traditional structures—in my case, a few in the prison and jail system—on occasion impacted our efforts to control career criminals and their connections to prison and street crimes.

Status quo policies empowered those whom the justice system was designed to control. Trying to revise an institutionalized structure in a large state or federal institution like the prison system and jails or any other institution is not a story of intrigue, heroism, or bravery on the part of those working on the inside. Instead, the example I give you concerns the power play implemented by some who resist change by outsiders and even legislative inquiries. It shows competing authority and the lengths some will go to control, invalidate, and work against a contributing agency partner on what should be a common goal for everyone in law enforcement.

This event will cover what was personally directed at me. It will also protect the official locations and identities of the persons involved where this occurred. Policing in any governmental agency is a competitive and sometimes jealous undertaking. The ego-driven nature of some authorities can get in the way of critical, collaborative work by those working inside to maintain order.

In law enforcement, the stakes are high. Policing is not a one-on-one game, then on to the next one, or a one-time firefight; it's a 24/7, 365 days a year, potentially life-and-death struggle. Competition across units within the justice system is a good thing that can lead to promotions and rewards, but from my point of view, the competition within the system should not thwart the efforts of professionals at any level. The criminal justice professional should be in competition with the criminal element; we are in there to stop the crime the career criminal and organized gangs can produce inside the institution and outside through willing opportunists who carry out his orders. Therefore, the career criminal should be our sole focus; anything else is just political drama.

In 1992, I became involved in such a drama; I was promoted to sergeant with the Arizona Department of Public Safety (AZ DPS), so I remained in the Intelligence Division, where I started supervising the Analysis Unit. This was followed by a few short months in Internal Affairs. But I kept my hand in monitoring prison gangs while assigned to the AZ DPS Intelligence Division gang squad. As a result, I was very well aware of the threat posed by Arizona's growing prison gang population and its expanding connections with other organized criminal groups.

One of the two Mexican American prison gangs had grown exponentially throughout the Arizona Department of Corrections (AZDOC) prisons. They are referred to as the New Mexican Mafia. My focus was clear after all the years of working with and tracking prison gangs beyond their reputation outside the prison system. Initially, I (as well as many in the law enforcement community) knew little about these predators. As a result, when gang members were released onto the streets, local law enforcement had no idea who they were or the threat these career criminals posed to the public. While incarcerated, these new recruits learned new tricks as though they had finished grade school and had completed lessons at the crime university in planning future actions. So, I tasked the Analysis Unit with constructing a New Mexican Mafia workbook, a "who's who" in an eight-and-a-half by five-in-a-half three-ring binder. The brown paper cover displayed a picture of the New Mafia tattoo. The project was labor-intensive and took weeks to finish.

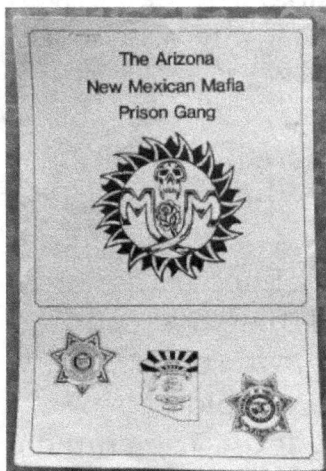

The Arizona
New Mexican Mafia
Prison Gang

Our exceptional team of civilian analysts had to construct a separate factsheet for each criminal member. In addition, each member required a complete criminal history check, listing felony convictions and biological information. Prison photographs were requested from the AZ DOC along with monikers and other gang identifiers. DPS picked up all costs for the binders and printing. I don't recall the exact number but I'm thinking around 100 books were published and distributed statewide to Arizona law enforcement agencies.

I found it hard to believe that someone would make a decision to discard this valuable information. I personally delivered a few dozen copies to a division within the AZ DOC. As a result, Operations staff, including the wardens, now had a tool to identify members of the expanding New Mexican Mafia membership. As new prisons were built, Mafia recruitment was taking place statewide.

Unfortunately, some within DOC leadership didn't see the need and the efforts put forth by DPS to aid them with the books on the inmates who posed the greatest threat to staff and inmates. Unfortunately, the books were later found stashed in a closet at DOC headquarters and never distributed to the staff who desperately needed them.

Knowing full well that it puts DOC employees at greater risk. It was as though a couple of supervisors within the DOC didn't want to see the depth of the growing prison gang problems that had become epidemic. My best conclusion was it had to do more with a particular administrator who did not care for me and this was his way of dismissing anything I was involved with. Crime was spreading like an untreated virus. I do not hold this error against the DOC organization just because a few administrators choose to let personal animosity interfere with doing the right thing to meet their commitment to the public; to think otherwise is amiss.

However, I understand how dangerous an unfortunate administrative decision can become as criminal activity plays out on the streets. Not using relevant data on career criminals blinds those in power to a real threat lurking in every prison as well as in local communities. This obstructionist behavior could have impacted the safety of all AZ DOC employees. Ultimately, the obstructionists' behaviors only encouraged my persistence in dealing with the threat of organized criminal groups in prisons. These bogeymen appear when new ideas result in acknowledgment for personnel who threaten the power or position of the administrator. Perhaps you experience these same bogeymen in your work environment.

The GITEM Legacy

During this same time period, I recognized the growing, largely unchecked threat presented by prison gangs connected to street gangs. The majority of those I had identified and profiled who belonged to prison gangs, of all races, had once belonged to a street gang or were tied to an ideology prior to their adult incarceration. This was especially true with Mexican American inmates and a growing inmate population of Mexican Nationals who, by then, had formed their own street gangs. I set out to design an intelligence-driven concept with multi-agency enforcement teams. After extensive research and consultation with police and corrections professionals, I submitted my flow-charted organizational model (written on large butcher block paper from my kitchen table) to DPS Intelligence Division commander, Captain Mike Denney, followed later by Captain David Gonzales. It was an innovative concept, one that could be operationalized by the state legislature as well as the law enforcement community.

Mike, a visionary, wrote a professional proposal and led the concept by successfully creating an intelligence-driven, statewide, multi-agency gang enforcement effort known as the Gang Intelligence and Team Enforcement Mission (GITEM). There is much I could say about Mike. One of the best tributes I can express professionally is that he always wanted to be in the field with the troops. He led from the front. More importantly, how could I not mention Mike as the person who introduced me to my wife way back at Cochise College in 1971? That was the best reward I've ever received.

GITEM grew into DPS's statewide multi-agency task force, taking on organized Criminal Street and criminal prison activities. GITEM became operational in 1994 as the street gang problem magnified across several western states. Gang activity impacted the greater Phoenix area severely, as well as rural parts of the state. Street gangs were operating openly in both rural and urban neighborhoods, but the damage was felt most severely in minority Hispanic, black, and Native American communities. The reciprocal effect flowing from California gangs invading Arizona and New Mexico was noticeable in the streets.

Originally, GITEM comprised four enforcement squads supervised by a DPS sergeant in Phoenix.

Squads consisted of officers from various agencies who were assigned to GITEM. Each squad could work in a city or location near or within Maricopa County that posed a street, prison, or motorcycle gang problem. Others worked together in locations saturated with gang activity and violence. GITEM expanded to Tucson, then had coverage statewide. I was one of its original sergeants who also monitored prison gangs.

Through the Arizona Legislature, GITEM was granted appropriations funding for a statewide multiagency enforcement task force. The Task Force's mission was to assist criminal justice agencies in enforcement efforts and collect and disseminate criminal gang information. We gave officers training regarding the identification and interdiction of gangs. In addition, GITEM supported problematic schools with reported gang activity and assisted community outreach programs. There was none better to fill these roles than Detective Charlie Ruiz, who specialized in working in Hispanic barrios and was a great gang officer.

GITEM eventually added an undercover squad led by Sergeant Andy Vasquez that penetrated several gangs, resulting in arrests for drug and weapons violations. Years later, GITEM added a gang immigration enforcement component. GITEM received awards from the International Chiefs of Police Association (ICPA) and the International Outlaw Motorcycle Gang Association (IOMEGA) for its innovative concept and results. GIITEM is still active today, but agents are working with dramatically reduced manpower and resources.

Indeed, GIITEM is an example of what can be done when like-minded criminal justice professionals, administrators, and legislatures come together to purposely solve problems. This multi-level policing model has positive effects on crime at the street level, and it controls career criminals who, though incarcerated, still jeopardize the safety and security of citizens in our communities.

I'm thinking out loud now: this same innovative assessment and action are needed on a broader national and international scale to meet the threat the Mexican cartels pose at the southern border.

Some time ago, as I started this memoir journey, I found myself in a rut. I began to wonder if anyone would be interested in what I had to say. I thought, "I am not a celebrity, athlete, politician, or someone of notoriety." I then purchased Steven Pressfield's book (my favorite author) *Do the Work*: "The Answer Is Always Yes." He wrote, "When an idea pops into our head, and we think, No, this is too crazy,"----that's the idea we want to share."

That is precisely how I felt when I started writing the GITEM concept, the Narcotics Strike Force proposal in the 1970s, the National Major Gang Task Force concept with Dale Welling, Gang Member Identifying Criteria, and other projects I was initially involved with. Indeed, the GITEM project and others are examples of lessons learned. Ideas and visions have no boundaries or interferences, and yes. It doesn't matter one's rank, title, socioeconomic status, color, or gender. Get the idea out of your head and write it down. Do you think I am not experiencing the same vibe as when I wrote this?

CHAPTER 6
THE REALITY OF LESSONS LEARNED

Prior to my prison task force assignment, I had over a dozen years' experience working in patrol, narcotics, investigations, and intelligence. I had experienced a variety of unique scenarios that occur in a jail custody setting. I conducted traffic stops, participated in search and arrest warrants, engaged in undercover operations, conducted surveillance, encountered shootings, and assisted with narcotics enforcement while working on intelligence assignments.

Yet, despite all these experiences, I was naïve about the criminal mindset within prison cultures. Each has its own personality traits, pecking order hierarchies, learned propensities, and even persuasive social skills in a prison setting. To educate myself, I devoured forensic content books about the criminal mindset. Learning about prison culture can be compared to an anthropologist's studying wild mustang herds or a lion tribe; each cultural species with its sub-subspecies follows unique behavioral patterns.

From the onset of my assignment in prison gangs, I devoted extensive personal study time and research to exploring the mindset of sociopathic, psychopathic, and antisocial-personality disorders. Why? Because the majority of those I encountered exhibited at least some of these character traits. All repeat criminal offenders had prior violence and assault records and exhibited disdain for authority. I realized I needed a deeper understanding of tribal-association behaviors. I became aware of the "us vs. them" mentality that spawned group dynamics within a set culture.

My collective studies greatly influenced my convictions about criminal mindsets because most of the people I dealt with exhibited a variety of traits and characteristics associated with antisocial and narcissistic disorders. They were repeat offenders, career criminals who had honed their expertise on the streets. Those facing release learned tricks from those they met in the prison yard. Once released, they were more educated and more likely to reoffend.

The First "Real" Career Criminal Encounter

Before any of my previous writings occurred, I want to share my first encounter with a "real" career criminal that opened my eyes for things to come in my career. Very few of these types of inmates made it into the Coconino County jail; they were an anomaly. In the early 1970s, Flagstaff was a quiet, sleepy little city, with its population coming from the university, recreation, and people on vacation on the way to the Grand Canyon, and mountain attractions. Flagstaff today is a larger city, and it sits on the direct route for drug smugglers headed east with narcotics from Mexico.

I would be remiss for not going back to tell you about this career journey. I remember it as if it were yesterday. Soon after starting my law enforcement career, I had my first real encounter with a career criminal, the "for real type" of career criminal. It occurred in the early 1970s while I was attending Northern Arizona University. I was at NAU in criminal justice studies while working as a reserve deputy with the Coconino County Sheriff's Office in Flagstaff, Arizona. Working in jail one weekend, I was told by one of the detectives that they had arrested a subject for an armed robbery.

The jail staff was informed that this subject had been arrested for armed robbery and had recently been released from San Quentin prison in California. He was 6'2", lean, and had some of the light blue eyes I've seen often since. Once he was civilized enough to talk to me, he drilled me with those eyes. He stood in front of his cell, always with something derogatory to say. I, in turn, would think about things I would like to do to him. He was sleeved up, with tattoos up and down his arms. He had an extensive criminal history, was considered dangerous, and was an alleged affiliate with the Aryan Brotherhood, the (AB) prison gang that was forming from California. So, we were cautioned to be very careful in our dealings with him.

During my time assigned to the jail, this inmate proved to be more than a handful. He was continuously disruptive and intimidating, stirring the other inmates to act out. I don't recall the reason. Perhaps he had plugged up his toilet and flooded his cell out of an act of defiance. But on one occasion, we had to do a forced cell entry to refrain him and place him in isolation. As soon as we opened his cell door, he fought us all the way, and it took several jail staff to subdue him enough to put him in handcuffs and place him in an isolated cell away from other inmates. I believe even the Sheriff himself was present. He was eventually sentenced to the Arizona Department of Corrections and became affiliated with the Arizona AB. Years later, I dealt with him while working in prison gangs.

At that time, I knew very little about the Aryan Brotherhood, prison gangs, or career criminals. But I wasn't naïve enough not to realize he and they must all be bad dudes. I'd been around bad dudes before, and you will hear about them. Those not exclusive to the criminal side.

The Threat They Pose
Engaging these threatening adversaries directly, whether they be career criminals, political terrorists, or drug cartels, with personnel and fiscal resources requires an uncompromising, costly, and proactive, committed effort. More importantly, it requires direct action—unrelenting, not red lines. Career individuals within organized groups, locally, nationally, and globally, make crime, terror, and power a profitable way of life. They are bent on acts of corruption, destruction, creating fear, and death. They are located anywhere and everywhere and are in every country. At the top of the hierarchy, are those calling the shots and making the decisions. They hire and pay "associates" and "proxies" to commit terror and crimes and create upheaval. Those giving orders have mastered their trade; they are working in the shadows and giving orders, oftentimes, from inside our state and federal prisons and across global border boundaries.

Those working with these groups have a steep learning curve to tie together the many threads composing their work. In my case, one would assume that my previous experiences would have given me a complete understanding of deviant criminal behaviors, but I admit that it took me years to gain this understanding. Therefore, I worry that law enforcement officials and other government agencies have not studied this problem in depth. May I be wrong? I do not hold that state and federal legislators close their ears and eyes to these costs with malice intentions. Many for whom we vote do not come from backgrounds in law enforcement, the military, or intelligence. They grew up in safe environments where criminal and extremist elements were not a threat. Accordingly, they have not been exposed to individuals who exhibit extreme anti-social, violent, and predatory psychological behaviors and dangerous, violent ideologies. They believe such forces will not come their way in their secure environment and gated communities; they are mistaken. It is often a case of out of sight, out of mind. Crime and criminals have a long reach.

Exemptions to this avoidance and naive mindset are individuals who have participated in law enforcement, military service, operational strike forces, US Marshal Fugitive Service, military special forces operations, and intelligence functions in special covert collection operations dealing with career criminals, including those who have worked long-term in deep undercover or intelligence assignments. These officers and operators, working while deep within an organized criminal group, some alone, have filled in the details for the whole picture. A great example is related by Alcohol Tobacco and Firearms (ATF) Agent William "Billy" Queen in his book *Under and Alone while undercover with the Mongol Outlaw Motorcycle Gang*. He will not tell you, but he was confronted at a time—life or death—by violent, overwhelming enemy forces deep in the jungles of Vietnam long before he was recognized in his ATF role that made the Mongols look like choir boys.

The Career Change to Corrections

Upon retiring from DPS in 1996, I began a different career path in corrections. I was hired to assist in creating and supervising a new Security Threat Group Unit (STGU) with the Arizona Department of Corrections, ADOC. Specifically, we dealt with the threat of organized gangs within a confinement setting. As supervisor of the STG Unit, I and my team implemented a new automated gang data system called the Gang Related Inmate Tracking System (GRITS).

Today, I do not know its title. We coordinated efforts with the Information Technology Division, ITD. Unfortunately, when I took this idea to a certain administrator, believe it or not, who showed up again? The obstructionist. This much-needed, valuable gang tracking automated tool was met with disapproval by a certain administrator above me in the chain of command. He did not, nor could he give me a reason why the organization would not benefit from its implementation; I could not believe it. Because I felt the need for this system was so great, I worked secretly with the ITD Director, who truly believed we needed it. It would be difficult to describe the reaction I received when he found out. Know this: I was not sure if paramedics would be needed due to his anger. This administrator was a person who always got his way. I knew my days were numbered with the AZ DOC.

In spite of this bump, we were able to create a formal written STG validation policy approved by the ADOC Director and begin validating suspected prison gang members. Through the validation process, prison gang members could be placed in the new state-of-the-art Special Management Unit. They were placed indefinitely, or until they renounced their gang membership. It was a means to remove prison gang members from the rest of the prison population to diminish their threat and influence. New prison policies supported the ADOC STG Unit, and newly created Special Security Units (SSU) within the prisons were implemented much like the California Department of Corrections and Rehabilitation (CDCR) Investigative Services Unit. The Special Security Units, monthly intelligence sharing meeting concepts ran parallel, but on a smaller scale than the California CDCR and CPGTF concept.

Out on the streets the Special Service Unit (SSU) was integral to the California Department of Corrections and Rehabilitation (CDCR), separating the most hardcore inmates, gang members, and parole violators. The unit is staffed by special agents assigned to offices throughout the state. Although the special agents work for CDCR, they are neither correctional officers nor parole agents. SSU special agents are full-time peace officers per the California Penal Code.

SSU agents, working closely with other law enforcement agencies, conduct criminal investigations involving prison inmates and state parolees on the street. They monitor prison gangs, gather criminal intelligence, and conduct narcotics enforcement. The Investigative Service Unit is a component within

CDCR adult prisons throughout California that conducts criminal investigations. The unit communicates with CDCR Investigative Services Units (ISU) and Institutional Gang Investigators (IGI), both working within the prisons, to validate the status and share information on prison gangs and security threat groups (STG).

But there was much more to come.

In December 1997, I left the Arizona Department of Corrections as the supervisor for the STG Unit. The Secretary (Director) of the State of New Mexico Corrections Department (NMCD), Robert Perry, asked me to come to New Mexico as an administrator to establish a Security Threat Group, the STG Unit. The Secretary wanted an STG unit like the Arizona Department of Corrections. Secretary Perry had a no-nonsense, get-the-job-done attitude; he wanted to control a serious gang problem deep-rooted in the NMCD prison system.

When I accepted this position, I understood the New Mexico Corrections' reputation for having some hardcore inmates. I planned to stay for a year and get the STG unit off the ground. I left my wife and home in Arizona; my children were grown, so I did not have plans to relocate to New Mexico. The NMCD upper management was quite generous; they provided a vehicle and a place to live for free. I was housed on prison grounds in married housing at the maximum-security prison in Santa Fe, New Mexico, referred to as NMCD Penitentiary.

The administration also allowed me to go home whenever time permitted. It was a convenient one-hour flight from Albuquerque to Phoenix. I did not have plans to relocate to NM, only to stay a year to ensure the STGU Unit was performing. The first few months entailed writing the new STGU policy and procedures for his approval. STG certification guidelines and gang member validation criteria a formal interview process for STG staff allocations took place, as well as procuring equipment and special uniforms. There was a two-week specialized training for the new STG Unit personnel; trainers were brought in from the California CDC and elsewhere to assist.

However, working in the NMCD initially presented some unique challenges. I had never been to New Mexico, so I was starting from scratch to understand the culture. The only person I knew was Secretary Perry. The initial reception I received from a large contingent of prison line staff was distant and aloof. I did not know how much the personnel in the NMCD tended to work as one collective; members were somewhat distrustful of outsiders.

A saving grace came from a friend from the Colorado Department of Corrections, Administrator of Classification Division, and Daryl Vigil. Daryl knew New Mexico culture, so he provided me with insight and encouragement. We were also board members of the NMGTF. Later, Old School Lieutenant Steve Lucero, whose assignment was working intelligence, became a confidant as well. Uniquely, I met a different inmate attitude and atmosphere in the NMCD prisons than I had felt in other correctional facilities in Arizona, California, and other states as well. I believe a lingering shadow of mystique hung over the state prisons, perhaps due to the 1980 violent prison riot, one of the worst in United States history.

As strange as this may sound, it felt as though the inmates, especially older inmates, bore this horrific event as a badge of honor, as part of the prison's history and allure. I have much respect for officers who continued working after the riot, especially after what they experienced. They continued to endure working in that environment.

Most reassuring to me when I arrived was the backing of the NMCD administration. They realized the inmate population had grown rapidly during the years preceding the riot. They lacked a policy to deal with a growing prison gang problem. They also recognized a bitter rivalry between two Hispanic prison gangs, the Syndicato Nuevo Mexico (SNM) and Los Carnales (LC). As a consequence of this rivalry, several murders had occurred, and there were increasing incidents of assault.

After a couple months, we finally got down to the business at hand, which was the validation process for inmates suspected of belonging to a prison gang. At this point, the four major prisons for NMCD had an STG team in place to validate an inmate as an STG member for placement in 24-hour maximum-security housing indefinitely; the only way out to a lower classification in the general population was to debrief or disassociate from the gang.

A portion of SNM and LC were in lockdown, but many members were unidentified and remained in medium custody in open prison yards. That provided them the freedom to recruit new members and actively pursue criminal activities. Before the STG Units' inception, the NMCD policy for placing inmates in lockdown status was based on behavior. It was not a policy that included gang membership. Rather, it is based on the decision and determination of the prison Warden. Things changed once the STGU started validating inmates in each of the prisons. It became a matter of our will and force over the gang's resistance. To be blunt, it was a Herculean task. The gangs were pissed off. The STG Unit was met with verbal and physical resistance from gang members at every turn.

The NMCD STG inmates were not used to being confronted and singled out by an assertive, dedicated team committed to taking the prisons back from their influence. We conducted massive cell searches looking for gang indicia. Pulling inmates out of their cells to photograph their gang tattoos often required additional staff assistance. The STG Unit concentrated efforts on intercepting illegal contraband. We initiated a robust effort in phone monitoring and reading mail. The team used all the new training and procedures to validate STG as gang members.

The Personal Retaliation-New Mexico

Over twenty years have passed since my time in New Mexico. It is safe to say that with time, memories fade across the many chapters of life. Before I began to relate these events, I remembered a file I kept entitled The Threats with the New Mexico Corrections Department. The NMCD STG Unit personnel wrote all the memoranda in reports. These memoranda helped me retrieve dates and facts that revealed the following:

In February 1998, one of my officers assigned to the STG team at the Penitentiary prison in Santa Fe told me he had interviewed a source to obtain some serious information. He wrote a memorandum on the interview that outlined threats to staff personnel and to me. Because of the serious nature of this data, his interview was followed up by a second interview. Deputy Warden, the Santa Fe STG Unit Coordinator, and I were present at the second interview. The source was a California out-of-state transfer classified as an associate with the Mexican Mafia on keep-away status. The source began the interview by saying I had helped him with a situation he faced in California so he was returning the favor.

Before receiving this information, a couple months earlier, Sergeant Richard Valdemar of the Los Angeles Sheriff's Department, assigned to the FBI Violent Gang Task Force in Los Angeles, called me. Richard was a friend, a highly esteemed, respected officer. Richard told me he was conducting a long-term Racketeering Influenced and Corrupt Organization (RICO) investigation against the California Mexican Mafia. He asked me if I could assist him in transferring this inmate to hide him from a critical threat. This inmate was important as a confidential source (CI) in the investigation in Los Angeles. The CI was a witness for the prosecution. There was a potential threat to the CI, so his relocation was paramount.

I then informed the NMCD classification administer, relating the circumstances. Shortly afterward, the CI was brought to the NMCD; he was housed in the Santa Fe Penitentiary Prison Administrative Security Facility.

Described in the memorandum, the CI related, "They know your name." (This statement was directed specifically at Frank Marcell.) CI proceeded to say, "I think x__ and x___ (Shot callers) are behind it. (referring to inmates)_x___, and _x___. (CI said they refer to him (Marcell) as "Little Frankie.") CI said, "This guy, the one they call "Inmate X," is the main *vato*. He is in Tucson or elsewhere on parole... He also mentioned that the names _x and __x, who brought him into the EME (New Mexican Mafia out of Arizona), __x__, and Inmate X's brother are the ones supposed to "gun down Paco." (The CI addressed Mr. Marcell as Paco.) CI stated that they had spotted him or surveilled Paco in Scottsdale or Mesa three weeks before." The memo said that the SNM and the Arizona New Mexican Mafia were communicating. That was jaw-dropping information.

After receiving this specific threat, I knew Richard and the prosecution team had thoroughly vetted him as a witness in the RICO investigation. These allegations told us that precautionary measures should be taken. At the conclusion of this interview, I contacted an investigator with the Arizona DOC STG Unit who used to work for me. I told him what we heard and asked if he would contact the parole office to see if the person of interest mentioned by the source was on out-of-state parole status from New Mexico to Arizona. We also verified this inmate's name and status through the NMCD records. He quickly got back to me and confirmed that the man in question was an out-of-state transfer who had violated parole; they were looking to pick him up.

I confirmed that I had been home on the weekend, as claimed by the CI. My wife and I went out for dinner at a restaurant near Scottsdale. If this were true, I was sure they would not have followed me from my home. I made it a habit to check my surroundings when leaving my residence, but it's still very concerning. I contacted a police supervisor from the city I lived in within Maricopa County and informed him of the circumstances. I asked if his department could put an extra patrol in my neighborhood. I did not tell my wife the full details. I just advised her that something had come up pertaining to me and that she should lock the doors at night and be extra vigilant wherever she went. We had been together long enough she knew what I met without asking more. I had no doubt that if the threat was real, it was me they were looking at, not my family.

One month later, Joe Romero, the STG Unit supervisor from the Central New Mexico Prison facility south of Albuquerque, conducted a six-hour STG debriefing interview. The inmate was an active member of the SNM who wanted to renounce his membership. He related that he felt his life was in jeopardy. He recounted how the SNM had attempted to hit him on previous occasions. We wrote a lengthy confidential debriefing pertaining to this threat information. The NMDC Administration was verbally briefed, and the information was disseminated across their level of authority.

The STG Unit supervisor provided a further verbal briefing related to the fact that two leaders of the SNM reportedly discussed plans to hit the "Arizona Guy," stating the gang program was interfering with their business. He said they believed "the Guy" lived in, or stayed at, the Academy Dormitory grounds in Santa Fe, New Mexico. He also mentioned two others who were affiliated with the Arizona New Mexican Mafia. He added that one of them had allegedly commented that he knew of the "Arizona guy" when he was involved in the STG program while incarcerated in Arizona. This was the second piece of information from sources that referenced attempts to locate me where I lived in New Mexico. We also confirmed the names of these inmates and personal events as told by both inmate sources.

The excerpts I cited were taken from the memorandum written by the STG Unit supervisor, saying what the sources revealed: I have chosen to use inmate X to replace the inmate's name and moniker in the reports. I do not know the status of these inmates today and do not want to place them or others in jeopardy. I had only been in New Mexico for a few months when we received both threats. However, these threats and related circumstances required special consideration. I was also aware that it was announced in one of the local newspapers after my hire where I previously worked and the formation of a new unit to address gangs within the prisons. Do you think the NM DOC inmates had an idea as to what would come?

Then, again, in September 1998, an STG Unit officer interviewed an inmate housed in the Santa Fe prison security housing unit. In the officer's subsequent memo, he mentioned that he had interviewed an out-of-state transfer inmate from California.

The CI stated that he had been incarcerated in other state correctional departments and had intensive knowledge of how STGs operated. He said the SNM was in the planning stage of ascertaining the address of and conducting hits on the staff of the NMCD. He also related much of the same information previously reported. However, it is unclear if the interview was conducted with the original source by another of the STGU officers or if this inmate was another independent source. The source's name was not mentioned in the memorandum for his protection. Because of the serious nature of these threat allegations, we hurriedly tried to collect and assemble written or verbal documentation not previously documented and collated from all the prisons into a central file. In doing so, there may have been some confusion about the interview date as opposed to a date on which the report was later written.

In either case, the source said he had an association with the California Mexican Mafia and had been given orders to keep the Sureños in check since there were rumors that some had been affiliating with known SNM members. The source stated there was a lot of talk about the STG program. He also mentioned that the inmates know the full name of the STG Coordinator, Frank Marcell. The inmate also stated that the SNM knew that Frank Marcell had previously been home to Arizona.

From October to December 1998, I don't have documentation that states that additional threat information came up. Then, in December 1998, we learned that the Phoenix FBI Violent Gang Task Force had arrested three Arizona New Mexican Mafia members for an alleged plot to kill the Arizona Department of Corrections Director, Terry Stewart. It was reported that they planned to hit the director at a restaurant, but the attempt was foiled when FBI Violent Gang Task Force members intervened. The Task Force had information concerning threats to Director Stewart, so they were targeting these subjects before their arrest.

In New Mexico, we were dealing with our own threats, mostly unaware of the specific investigative efforts concerning Director Stewart.

I was aware that the Arizona New Mexican Mafia, as well as the other STG groups in ADOC, were not thrilled with the validation program enforced by Director Stewart. To his credit and eventual safety, he had taken a hard line and would not back away from the policy measures he implemented. I applaud Director Stewart for his steadfast stance he took at personal peril. Inmates expressed this same hostility in New Mexico. As the original supervisor of the Arizona SIG Unit in the ADOC, I knew these hostilities existed. My involvement was widely known among the inmates. Based on my many years working prison gangs with the Arizona DPS before coming to the AZ DOC, I was concerned that if an alliance had been made with the SNM and the Arizona New Mexico Mafia, both would have a motivation for retaliation. After all, we were dealing with the mindset of prison gangs made up of career criminals.

I spent two years with NMCD. The STG Unit had accomplished much in its first year. However, there was still work to do. In my second year, the NMCD contracted with a private prison company and opened a new prison facility in Hobbs, New Mexico. Many inmates, including several validated SNM members, were transferred to fill that inmate population as required by the contract "to fill the prison population."

When the facility opened, it became a real problem for the STG Unit. The prison was located at the far southeast end of New Mexico, requiring some members of the STG Unit from the different facilities to travel great distances. The new Hobbs facility was plagued with inexperienced staff from its opening, a serious security concern. Incidences of ongoing assaults were increasing, and one murder had occurred.

I was tasked with sending the STG Unit to respond to gang or security issues at the prison. This meant I was routinely shuffling STG Unit officers there to help maintain security because of the ever-increasing tension at this prison. While these events were unfolding in New Mexico, at the same time, conspiratorial events in the AZDOC, the department I left, were also taking place. Undeniably, these occurrences were directly attributed to the creation of the STG policy. It was a clear and present threat to prison gangs in both states.

I was learning about retaliation—lessons known to those who have worked with a subversive group for any length of time. I was also aware that critical information is sometimes received piecemeal; during the heat of battle, information arrives one piece at a time. Until further corroborative information is known, you play the guessing game, as knowledge comes in dribs and drabs. Such information can initially be misleading, misconstrued, or misinterpreted, and the real significance might be questionable. The relevance of a bit of data is subject to an immediate tactical focus—the daily activity, not the big picture. The truth is assessed based on the knowledge of the person who obtains it or where and by whom it comes from.

Knowing this causes me to ponder: Are we now, our nation, and our governmental authorities overlooking, underestimating threats close to home, at our border with Mexico? Are we looking at the strategic long-term threat from both near and far? Does that international border line with Mexico suggest larger threats than Central/South Americans seeking work and safety in the US?

I began writing my account of crime and lessons learned in 2022. Sufficient time has passed for me to speak of the outcomes of that forewarned council. This massive, uncontrollable open border policy puts all reasoning, rationality, and ideology to the test. Immigration issues have surpassed debate. I am now more seriously concerned. Even disregarding earlier problems I previously referenced at the beginning of my writing on the Mexican Cartels, I ask, "How is it possible that elected government, military, and intelligence establishments sanction this level of threat to our economy and security?

Allowing unaccountable young single men of military age from foreign countries (many of whom are opposed to US democratic values) increases the danger. Immigrants are entering by the thousands each day; the recent escalation of individuals identified on the terrorist watch list also grows. Do we even know who is in our country to do us harm? This serious threat is beyond acceptable, agreed-upon national policy, political debate, and national controls, even discounting my prior experience working on and scrutinizing border issues. That was then; this is now.

Answering As for the threats against me personally while with the NMCD, who knows? I know there were great similarities in all the interviews conducted from different sources. We confirmed the validity of the names of the inmates mentioned as participants, including their hierarchy with the SNM. The conforming information obtained from two prison facilities indicated that word was passed among them. I will concede that the information about my commute to Arizona was most disturbing. How would they have known which weekends I was coming home? The information about being in Scottsdale in a specific weekend was unsettling. I was not in that city, but I was close by. Especially coming from an inmate source who was housed in the most secure and isolated facility in the state prison system.

I will say, at the time I was genuinely concerned that someone on our side, in New Mexico or Arizona, was working against me. I did not make a big deal about my apprehension. I kept my own council, and I don't recall if I discussed what was happening with any close friends outside of the NMCD. I was hesitant even to bring up this possibility. My concern was that certain Arizona law enforcement and corrections personnel would interpret it as trying to garner some kind of attention or status. In the end, comparing my situation to Director Stewart's, I certainly became much more vigilant. We continued to carry on with what our team was doing. It is now fair to say we were both threats to the prison gangs. Both Director Stewart's position as Director and mine, though different in authority and accountability, were certainly interfering with the activities of prison gangs in both states.

The Caution—They Can "Reach Out and Touch You"

Because of other demands at other prison facilities, sending the entire STG unit to Hobbs, New Mexico prison was becoming impossible. Aware of the prison environment and security risk, I did not want to send my personnel, one or two at a time, but my reservations were overruled. In reality, I was aware that the unit's attention was needed because of the overwhelming gang influence taking place. My reservations lie with the lack of adequate backup should a disturbance occur at that time. Much to my dismay, two STG Unit officers were attacked in a cell pod and overpowered. They held their ground by fighting with several inmates, back-to-back, long enough to reach a door out of the pod; the two came away with slight injuries. I felt guilty and responsible, wondering if I could have done more to intervene so they had not been sent to that location.

After two years, my time in New Mexico was coming to an end. The STG units were in good hands, up and running with proficiency. The constant grind of commuting from New Mexico to Arizona with never-ending demands on both ends took its toll. I wanted to come home. Before closing this chapter, I must recognize a few of the most loyal people who worked for me. Las Cruses Southern Correctional Complex STG Unit supervisor Jim Moore was there to cover my back in hostile situations. Annually, since leaving New Mexico, he has called to wish me a happy birthday. Such reverence blows my mind. I also recognize two STG Unit Supervisors, Danny Lucero and Joe Romero, and Paul

'Pablo' Martinez, who were loyal and had outstanding corrections credentials. Another of great assistance to me and loyalty came from Bernalillo County Sheriff's Office Detective Robert Martinez. Robert took a great interest in working prison gangs and often came to the penitentiary prison in Santa Fe, NM, to share information he had learned from the streets.

I share my time in New Mexico Corrections to provide examples of the commitment and length these predatory, highly organized groups go to when they perceive a real threat from law enforcement. I also want to describe the complexity of interpreting information in a fast-paced environment when data is collected from different sources and locations, often during a long-term intelligence collection process. Whether prison gangs, subversive terrorist groups, or cartels, the difficulty lies in collecting and analyzing information covering multiple locations, events, and subjects.

Many of these groups have learned the importance of compartmentalizing when planning an event, meaning A does not know who B is at each step in their planning stages to avoid detection. These groups are motivated for different reasons, but all are led by groupthink, "all for one and one for all." They have the means, resources, and pathological ability to reach out and touch you, so be aware.

At the close of two years with the NMCD, it was time to go home and back to Arizona. I did not want to return unemployed. I knew my time in New Mexico would count towards my state retirement and that I would be assured of keeping my health insurance. I hoped to procure employment somewhere in the Arizona justice system.

I contacted George Weisz, a friend I had known since the mid-1970s. I asked George if he knew of any job opportunities within Arizona. Back in the 1970's, George was a special agent with the Arizona Attorney General's Office (AAGO) and specialized in organized crime. He was active in several investigations into organized crime and was one of the primary investigators in the murder of reporter Don Bolles that created national attention, which long-tenured Arizonans would surely remember.

After that time and some 20+ years later, George retired, became a prominent Arizona congressman, and was then a senior adviser to Governor Jane Dee Hull. Over the years, George's accomplishments and leadership for the state of Arizona have been too numerous to list. Those of us who have followed the history of Arizona within the last five decades and know of George personally would agree.

George contacted me shortly after and said that there was a need for the Arizona Department of Juvenile Corrections (ADJC) to address juveniles within their system with ties to street gangs and the need to formalize gang-identifying criteria for custody classification. Further, he had procured a supervisory position and would work under the ADJC Director. Although I was grateful for this opportunity, I had mixed emotions. At the core of my being, I still desired to work for prison gangs, mixing it with the "big boys". However, I knew the door was shut with the ADOC. They had moved on in my absence and felt they had no need for my input or contributions. That's just the way things turn out, and they were probably right.

I left the NMCD in December 1999, a week before Christmas. I enjoyed a couple of weeks back home and began employment with the ADJC in January 2020. As things turned out, I was assigned under the assistant director of operations to supervise the fugitive apprehension team and task to create a standardized Gang Member Identifying Criteria (GMIC) system that came into existence while I was with the Prison Gang Unit back in the mid-1980s.

Although I felt a bit misplaced in the juvenile system, I was hopeful through my prior experiences, I could provide positive changes within the department. Again, my time with the ADJC was a short-lived six months as an opportunity arose that I felt fit my yearning, disposition, and opportunities better.

Though short-lived, I trained line staff at the ADJC reception centers to adopt the GMIC procedure for incoming juvenile offenders at the two juvenile facilities in Phoenix and Tucson. In addition, my time supervising the fugitive apprehension team was quite enlightening. I learned, and even surprised, as a juvenile, the cunning and measures they adapted to avoid the apprehension. All the while, I was still nosing around, trying to keep track of what the prison gangs were up to. Some habits are hard to change.

I cover this for two reasons, as it is part of my journey. I would like to personally thank George Weiisz for his kindness and thoughtfulness in giving me this opportunity to return to Arizona. Over the years, I have often thought I did not fully express my true appreciation to him. So, George, if you're reading this, my sincere thank you, and my friend; it's never too late. Second, it is a bridge to my time with the Maricopa County Sheriff's Office Detention Division. Having previously worked in jails and touring others nationwide with the law enforcement and corrections associations I belong to, it was a perfect fit.

The Jail Intelligence Unit

I came home to Arizona in December 1999. I was unaware that new, unexpected opportunities and adventures awaited me. In mid-2020, Deputy Chief of Intelligence, Steve Werner, asked me to assist in expanding and supervising a Jail Intelligence Unit (JIU) with the Maricopa County Sheriff's Office, MCSO, and Detention Division. Yes, working for the self-proclaimed "Toughest Sheriff in the Nation, Joe Arpaio." Maricopa County has the fourth-largest sheriff's office in the country; it houses over 7,500 inmates at all times. For almost nine years I worked there, the JIU was recognized nationwide. The unit gained respect from statewide law enforcement and federal agencies. If you come to my house, I will show you an autographed copy by Sheriff Arpaio of the pink underwear; it was distributed to every inmate in custody. I had mine framed and hung it on a wall in my home office.

The JIU was adopted by then Chief Deputy over the jails, Jerry Sheridan, who later became the Chief Deputy. In the nine or so years I was there. The JIU assisted with untold sensitive investigations and was known for disseminating information leads obtained in jails concerning outside agencies' investigations. Especially rewarding was the unit's involvement in assisting the Phoenix FBI Violent Gang Task Force preceding the arrest of numerous Arizona New Mexican Mafia members for Racketeering Influenced Corrupt Organization (RICO) charges. This investigation was led by Detectives Armando Saldate and Mike Maya from the Phoenix Police Department and assigned to the Task Force. The inmates were housed in the old Madison Street jail, where there were no isolated security cells of modern construction. Fortunately, that jail, no longer in use, was replaced by the 4th Avenue facility, a new high-security jail. In the old building, the lighting was poor. Each cell block had two tiers with large security glass fronts and a sliding door with bars to enter the pod. Approximately twenty Mafia or suspected members were housed in two pods next to one another within the cell block. Every day brought a new drama. The high numbers of known members with potential for violence or for plots and scams grew. Persistent antagonism within that cell block occurred daily. It was a housing security nightmare.

To manage this situation, the JIU initiated a special tactic to counteract aggressive behavior. I don't believe it had previously been tried, not in Arizona. We solicited assistance from several law enforcement agencies within Maricopa County and beyond, including the FBI Task Force. We asked if they could provide representatives from their agencies to participate with us in searches in the security housing unit occupied by the AZ Mexican Mafia.

These cell block searches were conducted randomly on a few different occasions. Each agency's represen-tative was asked to wear their unique raid jacket with the logo of their agency imprinted to distin-guish them from the county JIU-as-signed staff. The presence of many law enforcement agencies was over-whelming. It sent a clear message that

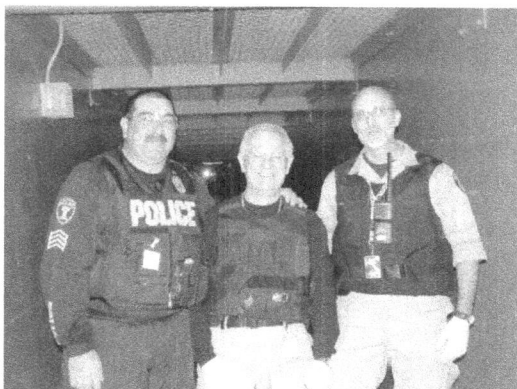

Arizona Gang Investigators Association President Chuck. Scoville, me and Ken Lucas. Cell search's at AZ DOC, Special Management Unit 11

our car club was bigger than theirs. Mafia members certainly did not like it, and the tactic did neutralize their behavior for a while—but just for a while. The results of these massive searches were so successful that the ADOC Special Management Unit 2, which held validated prison gang members, also conducted searches inviting law enforcement agencies to participate.

In 2005, the Madison jail was closed when the new four-story 4th Avenue jail opened, housing high (medium to maximum) custody level inmates. Most of the inmates from the Madison jail were moved to 4th Avenue. Currently, Level 4 is a maximum-security cus-tody unit with a state-of-the-art, high security design. It includes individual showers within a cell and a small exercise yard between two cells. This fourth level con-sisted mostly of known prison gang members, murder-ers, and other high-crime individuals. As secure as that jail was, at all levels, inmates were consistently finding ways to smuggle in drugs or other contraband.

I spent much time with the JIU team at Madison and 4th Ave. jails. It was a day-in and day-out routine to outwit the ingenious ways inmates can get drugs and other contraband inside or prevent assaults. Criminal-minded individuals will continue their criminal ways wherever they live; they just have a smaller playground to work within at the jail. JIU officers became especially proficient in source development, which greatly helped security. Many of the Jail Intelligence Unit personnel were young, energetic detention officers and employees eager to learn the craft of intelligence and apply it to career criminals. We were also assisted by a proactive and very intense Jail Response Team that greatly enhanced our efforts. Originally, Sergeant Janice Mallaburn supervised the original JIA unit, and as the JIU expanded, Lieutenant Valory Doss, Sergeants Javier Gilmore, Don Law, and I took on the job. Both Javier and Don were later promoted to Lieutenant. We were a team.

The Federal Project

My last assignment was as a founding member of the FBI/California Gang Intelligence Initiative (CGII), now called the Correctional Intelligence Task Force (CITF). This assignment would not have been possible without the approval and confidence of a longtime friend, author, and confidant, Brian Parry. By this time, Brian had retired from the CDC as Director of the Special Services Unit. He was hired and consulted with the

FBI on the national strategic strategies of subversive groups within the prison systems nationwide.

The CITF was established in 2010 to serve as a joint intelligence task force consisting of personnel hired from various agencies who had served in former careers. My assigned jurisdiction was Arizona and Nevada. The CITF partnered with the Federal Bureau of Investigations (FBI), the Federal Bureau of Prisons (BOP), and the California Department of Corrections.

Much of my work was in conjunction with the BOP monitoring STG activities. Because of the sensitivity and classification of the information, I am not authorized to go into detail. I also collaborated on many issues with my CGII counterpart, retired CDC SSU Agent Leo Duarte, stationed in southern California. His vast expertise in prison gangs, particularly the Mexican Mafia, was always informative, spot on and quite beneficial when attempting to vet source information. I also had the pleasure of working, almost daily, on subversive groups with one of the most talented individuals within BOP, Investigator John Finney. Thank you, John, for the experience of monitoring who was in the "mix."

The Emerging Career Criminal and Crime Today

This new type of criminal is adapting to revised social norms, which allow for a new variety of criminal activities (modus operandi). Judges giving lesser sentences than mandated by sentencing guidelines allow gangs and criminal-minded individuals to adjust their levels of crime to match the revised sentencing allowances. They are also adjusting their criminal activity to take advantage of changing police and prosecution policies influenced by lenient judges. Yes, they are opportunists and pioneers of a new era. But these career criminals are not less dangerous and destructive.

Am I alone in asking what criminal advances we are witnessing? And thinking, what is going on? I hope my words adequately describe what I perceive to be unfolding within the United States, specifically concerning crime and organized criminals' plans to thwart personal liberty and the US economy. I see the duality of two groups of people influencing the operations of the police and fighting crime.

There are also two types of criminal groups ascending on two fronts. There are two groups of citizens and politicians who stand in conflict: first, those who want to stop police from using their full resources and limit tax funds for policing. They believe that moving funds from local police departments and adding street counselors and after an arrest leniency facing a judge will cut down on street crime. The opposing, more conservative, traditional voice of citizens in crime-ridden cities is to increase funding for policing at all levels and to enhance tougher convictions. These two ideologies voice conflicting messages to legislators who hold the purse strings. You will have to make your own choice. I do know criminals do not care about opinions or political agendas; they will continue doing what they do best—crime.

When partisan political ideology, precepts, partisanship with untrained citizen groups, and parity take precedence over enforcing existing statutory criminal laws. While sentencing guidelines are arbitrarily selective, the criminal element will always emerge on top. This truth has alarming consequences, especially when organized criminal responses are suddenly implemented with crime sweeping across the country. Unfortunately, the general public is not aware of the tactical strength the justice system must then employ to secure order. This type of selective, soft marginalizing responses to overt acts of aggression and violence is definitely noticed by the military who are, and in the future will be, engaged in conflicts, confronting terrorist and insurrectionist organizations across the globe.

The two groups of new criminals account for a large portion of crime in America. I describe both groups as opportunists. However, the Cartels are far more sinister supplying wholesale death, leaving untold sadness and despair to those left behind.

CHAPTER 7
INFORMATION SHARING

In my early years of working in prison gangs, California was the only state with a formal system for sharing this *specific* kind of information. I knew this by attending the California Prison Gang Task Force (CPTGF) meetings. I discovered they disseminated timely intelligence-based information and analysis to members. The CPGTF members, in turn, made this information available to their respective agencies: street officers, detectives, feds, county jails, and correctional facility special services unit personnel.

I attended these meetings for 30+ years when I could. I, in turn, shared the information I gathered there with street and prison officers, detectives, feds, and local county jails in Arizona. The officers, agents and administrators I met along the way at CPGTF had tenured experience and showed a willingness to accept me as one of their own. It was all the incentive I needed in Arizona to pursue those committed to a life of crime.

I was compelled to try to do something about this gang crime wave in Arizona. I need to thank Dale Welling (US Parole), Lenny Lopez, Dan Beckwith, Gerry Kenyon (BOP), Brian Parry, Joe Delatorre, Leo Duarte, Devon Hawkes, Robert Marquez, Chris Miramontes, Mo Chavez (CDC), Richard Valdemar, Bill Philpot,

'Bubba' Williams (LASD), Mike Vaugh (RIP), Rich Duran (LAPD), David Contreras (SDPD), Sergeant Jim Brown from Folsom Prison, and many, many others who did this work. Thank you. I see your faces.

As part of this southwest history, we need to see the intelligence arena process and its evolution, including the CPTGF in the 1970s through today. The California Department of Justice, Intelligence, and Organized Crime Division authorities who were among the first national agencies to implement strict intelligence process guidelines. Their work incorporated the full circle of collected, corroborated information; they collated, analyzed, and disseminated this data into an intelligence product. After this process, the report was made available to authorities seeking information on persons of interest.

Thus, they could provide information on an offender's criminal history when requested. Similarly, yet using a different process, I later authored a concept called "Cradle to Grave," a collection plan for working officers to track offenders and provide them with a complete suspect profile from arrest through court, conviction, sentencing, prison, parole, and release to the streets. It also revealed more detail about an offender's particular offense and the escalation and history of criminal activity. I spoke at various training conferences, showing officers how to apply this process.

It is still critical for officers' safety concerns. They need to gather an intelligence portrait on a subject of interest. The concept never really got off the ground. Perhaps it required too much collection and collation of information. However, it was a valuable tool for me when profiling a suspect.

The Cradle to Grave Concept

MARCH 1997

bulletin

ROCKY MOUNTAIN INFORMATION NETWORK

8   RMIN BULLETIN   MARCH 1997

GRITS:

Tracking Gang Members Cradle to Grave

**by Frank "Paco" Marcell,
Arizona Department of Corrections STG Unit Manager**

At the national meeting of the RISS Gang Project meeting in Phoenix in February, Frank "Paco" Marcell presented his Gang Related Inmate Tracking System that, as he tells us here, he has spent 13 years formulating. What he doesn't tell us is that he poured a lifetime of personal and professional experience into developing this program. A product of a tough Los Angeles neighborhood, he realized his childhood dream the day he was sworn in a law enforcement officer.

It was only natural that he would gravitate to the gang beat. He knew how the streets and life in many neighborhoods could be run by gangs.

He conceived the model for Arizona DPS' now-nationally recognized Gang Intelligence Team Enforcement Mission. After 23 years, he retired and took a position managing the Arizona Department of Corrections Security Threat Group Intelligence Unit. There he saw the need for GRITS and responded with an innovative model for inmate tracking that links law enforcement agencies and corrections departments.

for law enforcement use only

Cradle to grave

131

The Influential Encounters

I make an exception for someone I need to recognize outside of the law enforcement field, but yet inside in so many ways. "Mundo" was the very subject of such research and scrutiny in his younger days. Ramon "Mundo" Mendoza, a former highly influential California Mexican Mafia member, gave me valuable insight into the mind of the criminal by his words and readings. Mundo did not realize it, but at a particular time in my career, I was asked to speak at a gang association conference about the career criminal; after I was done speaking, Mundo confirmed the accuracy of my insight. His acknowledgment and assurance kept me motivated—none better to be critiqued by. Since his redemption and salvation from that world, Mundo has been the author of several books; he is a national speaker, a trusted consultant, and a confidant to the criminal justice community and to me personally.

Another person came into my life through a gang conference in Colorado Springs. I had heard of him at the start of my prison gang assignment. When I finished speaking, a noticeable older man, dressed somewhat in old-school apparel and wearing a baseball cap, approached me. He had a look of determination and experience when he confidently introduced himself. He said, "I'm Bob 'Moco' Morrill with the Texas Department of Corrections. You were talking about Armando' Mandi' Varela; I was one of the founding members of the California PGTF." From that point on, the only name I called Bob was "Moco," (booger in Spanish) a nickname he earned during his career in California. It's a funny story that only he could tell.

Moco had retired from the Texas Department of Corrections and moved to Prescott Valley, Arizona. He authored *The Mexican Mafia—The Story and The Traffic Stop*. During the periods when Moco was writing, he occasionally came to my house to spend the night. We would take the old photos he used in his books to Walgreens to get enhanced copies. I introduced Moco to several of my law enforcement friends, and they got a kick from listening to his stories. A requirement was always to meet for breakfast at a Mexican restaurant serving chorizo and eggs.

Much can be said about Moco's law enforcement career in California and the controversy surrounding the aftermath of the 1977 traffic stop he participated in with the Monterey Park Police Department, involving two California Mexican Mafia members. Due to circumstances occurring before and after the traffic stop, law enforcement agencies drew conclusions regarding the legality and testimonies of those involved in that stop. The argument eventually reached the highest offices of politics in California and, to this day, may still be unsettled. I often heard Moco's side of the story as we enjoyed a glass or two, maybe three, of red wine. Moco introduced me to California Department of Corrections Parole Administer Tony Casas, and others, who I chose not to name, who vouched for Moco. Tony knew as much about gangs in prison as anyone I have met since then. In my mind, he was a legend. I also listened over the years to the implications and assertions of those attending the PGTF meetings about the controversy. The story was occasionally repeated, and all those involved had good intentions, but they were not there when the incident occurred. Neither was I, so I make no judgment as to Moco's story.

I spent a lot of time with Moco. So often, he expressed his remorse, anger, and sadness that haunted him after the traffic stop incident until his death a few years ago. We talked for hours about the Mexican Mafia, prison gangs, and related topics. I learned a lot from him; he made me laugh and took my teasing and nurturing. I miss him.

The Unlikely Alliance

My acknowledgment of Moco brings up something that has been gnawing at me concerning someone I thought of adding but rationalized it was not relevant to my message. My reluctance may have been based on others' perceptions of me. I believe this is what happened in Moco's situation. I began thinking through it with candor, and open-mindedness, digging deeper, and stepping forward to acknowledge this person. As some turned against Moco, that could also happen to me. It is a story of incidents within my journey. I knew of the controversy surrounding Moco as well as this next person of interest—I heard about it, even from friends. Still, I also know what it is like to be on the receiving end of those in positions of power and influence and those with their own agendas when they disagree with others' findings. We all like to think we're right and on the right side.

I'm over others' perceptions now, so I can tell you about another person who came into my life and was embroiled in a similar controversy. Over my career, it's been hard to fathom all the people I've known and met within the criminal justice system. Sometimes, things do not start out as you expect them to. They often end differently as well.

Mary Duran from Phoenix, Arizona, gained a reputation as one of the foremost mitigation specialists across the county in death-row cases, specializing as an investigator for the defense in homicide investigations. Mary was involved in many interesting ventures. She can be loud, swearing up a storm, confident, and confronting. I experienced all of it when she requested me for depositions.

Mary came into my life in the beginning, on at least three occasions, as I worked in prison gangs. Two of those occasions involved homicide investigations. The first encounter was in 1986 when I was notified and responded to a murder at the ADOC Perryville facility west of Phoenix. The victim was a suspected member of the NMM, whom I knew little about. This occurred at a time when rival Hispanic factions were going tic-for-tac on assaults and murders. Because of my presence at the crime scene, my name was put into the prison investigators' homicide report. Though there were a few likely suspects at the time, the case was not solved until later.

Sometime after the murder, I received a court order advising me I was scheduled for a deposition with none other than Mary Duran. In a deposition, you are sworn to tell the truth, and it's recorded and often videotaped. I was ordered to bring all intelligence reports, files, and the Mexican Mafia workbook I created. Mary had heard I had the notebook with me at the prison.

Until then, I had never met her, but I had heard talk of her being cordial with certain AB members and the AZ NMM. I had experience with the discovery issue process handled by defense attorneys, so I knew such broad requests were attempts to gain access to confidential intelligence files. Knowing this, I had created a working identification file containing mostly open-source information like a photograph, a rap sheet, newspaper articles, and physical and biographical information should such a situation arise. The ethical or legal question is, "Separate from confidential files, should these types of documents be requested?" When left with no other choice to produce confidential documents a request is needed with an in camera hearing with a judge to decide. In this case, I knew little to nothing about the victim other than he was said to be an associate of the AZ NM.

I did not take notes at the homicide scene. That was left to the prison investigators. Instead, I kept what I wanted to know in my head. I was also not carrying the AZ NMM workbook I have described in another section of the book, but instead a red memory finder notebook. I was not asked to produce that journal, so I would not mention it unless I was explicitly asked about a red book. The deposition was grinding. Mary kept pounding about the NMM workbook, saying she had heard I had it with me at the prison. She probed into many issues as to what I knew about prison gangs. My answers were short, conveying the bare minimum. No way was I going to be the one who gave up confidential intelligence files. From the beginning of working in prison gangs until this encounter. Her name would come up from other peers and sources who said Mary had inquired about me. I remember seeing her around, but she may not have seen me. At that time, in my mind and maybe hers, there was a distrust between us. It's the old adversary thing in this kind of business and working environment.

At one point, years later, Mary had become the victim of accusations from an AZ NMM member source who went public, accusing her of bringing drugs into the jail. This same source did not care for me, and I did not trust him. A few years later, his name came up in events with me while I was employed with the New Mexico Corrections Department. In all my years working for prison gangs, I never had a source tell *me* Mary was involved in illegal activities. Was I sympathetic to her situation? Yes, but that was to come later. In her soul, she is sort of like the Father Flanagan figure, who thought there was never a bad boy who could not change.

Another incident in which I faced Mary involved a murdered Aryan Brotherhood member who was killed by a shotgun blast on the streets. The murder was not solved immediately but was resolved a short time later. I knew of this subject from his time in prison. He was part of the wayward, up-and-coming membership. A confidential source had contacted me a day after the shooting and said that the rumor was that he had a conflict with the Dirty Dozen Motorcycle Club, so they retaliated. I reported this to the Phoenix Police homicide case detective, who was making the preliminary report.

Mary Duran was on the defense team and obviously obtained a copy of the preliminary report. The judge subpoenaed me to produce my confidential source and be interviewed by Mary. The reason for this deposition was based on the Brady rule, which mandates all exculpatory information must be disclosed, in particular with homicide investigations. Whenever I provided uncorroborated information to investigators, I requested them not to disclose my name unless necessary because it afforded me the anonymity to operate behind the scenes through confidential source information. In this case, my name and information, again, ended up in the initial case report as with the incident murder that happened at the prison. I could not disclose this source, a very close associate of the Aryan Brotherhood. This person feared for his or her well-being by talking to me.

I was very concerned for the safety of my informant. I wrote an affidavit to the judge via the county attorney's office outlining fifteen reasons I could not disclose this source. The judge ruled that the source would provide a telephonic interview with the source's voice disguised. Ultimately, the victim's former girlfriend and her new boyfriend returned, confessing that he had committed the crime. To my recollection the interview never took place. I still have a copy of the affidavit.

Much time passed before I got a call from Mary asking if she could speak with me privately. By then, I had retired from the AZ DPS and was working for the ADOC. I was guarded; she did not seem to be. We met on a bench near the parking lot at the ADOC headquarters. She gave me a heads-up on some very relevant information about safety concerns. Notably, this conversation allowed us to get to know each other differently and more personally. Reflectively, I now say Mary made me better at the seriousness of handling informants and my responses during the interviewing process by the defense counsel. She knew her business, and I knew I could not be caught slipping or giving misleading information.

Over the years, Mary and I have met and talked about many things. We don't always agree or interpret events in the same way. But I admire her tenacity and honesty; she is a stand-up lady. I know she believed in her clients and fought for them vigorously. Perhaps her concern for these individuals stems from her years as a very young woman in a Catholic convent, although she would never admit it. It has turned out to be the same way she believes in me. She is loyal.

If you are reading this and are familiar with the controversy with Mary, you might be unsettled because of things you have heard. Differences of opinion remain, especially when friends and associates are involved in such matters. I learned a valuable lesson that perceptions of "truth" and "right" are hard for outside observers to change. Nevertheless, a perceived adversary can become an ally if you see through the chatter.

The National Response and Expertise

Over the years of working in investigation and intelligence, I came to believe that state and national associations held the answer to solving training and information sharing needs. Here's why: For several years, I served as a board member for the National Major Gang Task Force, NMGTF, and the ILGIA, and I remained a member of the California Prison Gang Task Force, CPTGF. Few, outside of these police and correctional agency representatives, knew about the phenomenon of organized gangs in prisons. As members of these associations, we knew the impact and how incarcerated career criminals continued to reach out into the streets, with followers committing crimes directed by leaders behind bars. This knowledge, however, had not been adequately shared with law enforcement at all levels nationwide. There was a lack of inter-agency communication, and no forum existed to get the word out to the criminal justice community. Prison gangs formed naturally along race lines with career criminal leaders who were entrenched in most state-run prison systems and the Bureau of Prisons (BOP). This prison gang phenomenon was no longer isolated to California, Arizona, Texas, New Mexico, and BOP.

National accounts of gang-against-gang violence were mounting, assaults and murders were increasing, and the safety of correctional staff workers was at risk, along with the lives of cops and the public. The timing was perfect for the NMGTF to work as the vehicle providing training. So, we organized training conferences across the US with emphasis on Security Threat Groups, or STGs training; these attendee's representatives adopted policies as a formal concept by which prison administrators could remove predatory inmates from the general population and place them in special security housing.

My professional associates shared their stories, policies, and experiences about dealings with prison gangs and career criminals nationally. The NMGTF board members did not know how significant their contributions were to me personally. They were the experts, well respected in their jurisdictions.

As a result, through these associations, I met and learned about local heroes—individuals in the shadows, in unheralded workplaces within the corrections system—people who worked a tough beat and were instrumental in initiating positive changes that ensured the safety for employees and inmates.

Many good men and women with tremendous knowledge of the career criminal were on the NMGTF executive board, like Brian Parry and Joe Delatorre from the California Department of Corrections, "Big" Bill Riley from the Washington Department of Corrections, Lina Presley from Indiana, and Sammy Buentello from the Texas Department of Corrections. Ben Griego and Daryl Vigil from the Colorado Corrections were ahead of the pack in the classification and confinement of inmates involved in security threat groups. Their shared knowledge gave me some building block material I feel honored sharing with readers.

This same phenomenon occurred in Arizona, with attention to prison gangs in the 1980s. It seemed as though conservative Arizona was always the tail wagging the dog as our officers felt the negative effects of what was happening in California. At that time, the Phoenix Police Department had its gang squad, and DPS had assigned detectives to work for prison gangs; however, no central repository of information was collated, analyzed, or disseminated to law enforcement agencies throughout the state. With the exception of the DPS Analysis Unit, which produced prison gang identification books in the late 1970s and early 1980s.

Personally, way back in the early 1980s, before the Prison Gang Task Force and GITEM, while assigned as a detective, I could not visualize how this new assignment would allow me to work with prison gangs (Security Threat Groups (STG)) with the Arizona Department of Public Safety (AZDPS). The concept of interagency cooperation was, however, evolving. I was hopeful that Arizona could establish these specialized units to offer greater security to prisoners and prison employees. This is where my career path led me to this very specialized calling.

The Birth of the National Major Gang Task Force
How did I know this assignment in the early 1980's would lead to a lifetime career? It did not take me long to recognize that officer safety and public safety trumped any other consideration in dealing with career criminals in state prisons. I knew Arizona had to get a new outlook on its pursuit of criminal gangs that infiltrated local communities. This journey gave me valuable experience. I learned practical lessons, and my thinking evolved throughout my years in this specialized field. Eventually, I was promoted to supervise street, prison, and jail gangs/intelligence units in Arizona and New Mexico.

As a board member, I became associated with the National Major Gang Task Force, NMGTF, and the International Latino Gang Investigators Association. This platform allowed board members and me from different states to provide quality consultation services for several correctional departments across the United States. Other state prison departments found it necessary to form their own gang/intelligence security threat group units.

It may be amusing to share with you how the

NMGTF concept evolved. If nothing more, it is an example of how unrestricted, inquisitive minds work in collaboration. In 1992, I attended a California Prison Gang Task Force, CPGTF, meeting in Orange County, California, at a hotel next to Disneyland. Following the meeting during a hosted hospitality hour, US Parole Officer Dale Welling from Sacramento, California, approached me, asking me to walk out with him. I did not want to go and would have stuck around to enjoy the libations and share the scuttlebutt of those working prison gangs. But knowing Dale, a respected CPGTF board member, I thought it might be something about CPGTF's internal politics he had to offer me.

The reason for my initial concern was the exceptionally dedicated, confident, and spirited nature of those who routinely attend the CPGTF meetings. They came from different agencies throughout California, from all levels of criminal justice departments. They handled the toughest assignment, dealing with their jurisdiction's most dangerous career criminals. They were highly competitive and carefully listened, assessed, and scrutinized the information a fellow representative put forth. They were not shy to say if information put forth was not vetted; when needed, they made efforts to confirm the data. The point I am making here is this: these specific organizations' representatives worked from the "ground up, hands-on"; that is what made them effective.

Upon leaving the hotel, Dale said, "Let's take a walk to Disneyland." My thought was, "As much as I like Disneyland, I did not go to the meeting to be entertained at the amusement park." I said nothing, but I thought, "What is this leading to? Is it about something he and

I had discussed previously?" Dale led me to a tram rail on the outside interior of the park; it took us above and around the exterior of Disneyland, offering a view of all the various adventures. I can guess what you may be thinking by now. But I knew Dale was a man of integrity, he knew the federal prison and parole system well and we had prior conversations about the importance of information sharing.

When we boarded the rail, we had a car all to ourselves. Dale opened the conversation to discuss the concept of a national organization. We discussed assembling board members across the US with experience working with gangs in a corrections setting. We visualized a forum through which national trends, policies, techniques, and training could be provided uniformly. If I told you we continued to ride around Disneyland several times, would you believe me?

A short time later, Dale was scheduled to speak at a training function in Tucson, Arizona, so I drove down from Phoenix to meet him. Over dinner, we picked up our conversation as if we were back on the tram rail. When we discussed a specific topic, I wrote it down on a napkin. Immediately, Dale would snatch it up and pocket it. We both knew we were on to something bigger than the two of us.

We were conceptualizing and planning what would become the National Major Gang Task Force, or NMGTF. Little did I know, Dale had been collaborating with the Bureau of Prisons, BOP, Intelligence Administrator Craig Trott, and Don Lyddane from the Federal Bureau of Investigation, who could carry the concept through the BOP and the Federal Bureau of Investigation, FBI. The association was founded in 1993 and received financial support and sponsorship from the Verizon Corporation. Dale became the first board president, and Craig and I became board members. Don, a retired Detective Sergeant with the Washington DC Police Department, was employed with the FBI Gang Safe Streets and our FBI liaison.

In 2008, we lost the sponsorship with Verizon, along with other internal issues; consequently, the NMGTF closed the shop in 2009, and the results of the NMGTF rest in history. Today, its recognition is hardly known, but its efforts were the catalyst nationwide to expose a career criminal element spawned in prisons with tentacles that reached out to local streets.

The International Latino Gang Investigators Association

A few years later, I became a board member of the ILGIA. This organization provides expertise and knowledge for the growing Hispanic/Latino gang epidemic problem nationally. Its founder and first association president was Gabe Morales, author of several books as a research specialist. On his podcast, Gabe interviews individuals in the criminal justice profession. You might be interested in looking this up.

The ILGIA is still active, and its membership has expanded into Mexico and Central America. These dedicated brother and sister peace officers do their duty in dangerous environments, combating ruthless criminal organizations yet unseen in the US. I wanted you, the reader, to know that associations like the ILGIA are still active; these organizations are not burdened by bureaucratic or political interference. The ILGIA hosts a yearly conference in Las Vegas, Nevada, for which they assemble speakers with expertise on a myriad of topics ranging from border issues to street and prison gangs and drugs, and they provide an up-to-date reality check of crime and criminals of Latino origin. As I write this, I must pause and convey my solemn regret for not having the means to mention each of my colleagues by name because of the web and the flow of new board members coming and going during the NMGTF's and ILGIA's existence.

For several years, I was fortunate to travel and interface with many of them across the United States as part of these vital professional associations. What is important is the fact that many organizations' representatives played a role in national decision-making relative to new gang and intelligence policies, procedures, and organizational concepts. Please know that my overwhelming concern is that I may have omitted someone unintentionally deserving of recognition.

The Cycle of Intelligence Unfolding
I was not satisfied with the lack of resources available in Arizona at that time. My assignment was in prison gangs with AZ DPS, so I became familiar with how California dealt with its prison, street, and confinement issues by attending the CPGTF meetings. I knew Arizona had been battling prison gangs for over a decade. I recognized how serious the problem had become, so I began to process the concepts needed in Arizona to enhance my proficiency.

I believe I can say that the various concepts I assisted with developing—those that were adopted— were proactive and preemptive. The most challenging thing during those early years was finding ways to examine criminals within the gangs from a distance. I wanted to know if it was possible to scrutinize them from the outside well enough to calculate their moves. Was it possible to evaluate the next criminal activity and assess its likelihood of threat when a released gang member confronted a law enforcement officer?

From the very beginning of my assignment, there was a person in ADOC I sought out, ran things by, trusted, and respected. He did not have a formal intelligence training background, but he knew the tradecraft intuitively. He specialized in HUMINT intelligence gathering, mano y mano, face-to-face with inmates from all races. He had historical knowledge about the on-set and evolution of these prison gangs. His experience, knowledge, and insight confirmed what I was expecting. This kind of first-hand, lived experience cannot be found in training manuals. He was old-school, country-style, and knew the convict world's players and bosses. He worked largely unheralded outside of the AZ DOC, except when things went really bad—like a murder in prison, an escape, or we needed information from the prison grapevine. Sergeant Mike 'David' Farley (I have learned) is like many dedicated professionals who do not seek the spotlight.

THE PROCEDURE

CHAPTER 8
THE OPPORTUNIST-GROUP ONE:
The Emerging Menace Today

Group One: Initially, this growing crime wave across cities was perceived by some as a reaction to issues of injustice by ethnicity, social class, and gender. It started as a movement or mindset spurred by a sense of immunity to the law. The opportunists lack concern for the consequences of unlawful acts. They feel "those laws do not apply to us, given our special circumstances." This is a self-imposed justification by some criminals with narcissistic thinking; they have a victimization mentality and an ideological belief that runs contrary to societal norms that ensure equal justice to all as defined by the US Constitution.

Specifics of race, gender, and crime patterns cannot singularly categorize all participants as young, middle-aged, white, black, or other race. This movement, a display of crime and purge, has rapidly ascended across too many large cities; each has its own demographic, which makes it impossible to put all crimes and their causes into one category. We know the movement has progressed intentionally. From the start of this movement, what appeared as protests and criminal acts by individuals appeared as a few thieves taking what they thought they deserved from a convenience store. Then progressing to groups targeting and looting stores in a mall is not an isolated case of "righting a social injustice." It is organized crime at work: mob mentality slowly destroying communities.

Group one is a homegrown phenomenon of noted diverse criminal participants. Crimes of convenience occur in easily accessible places. These "strike and grab" opportunists work as subversive groups to exploit businesses, rob and steal at will. Examples include raids on drug stores, shopping malls, and subway depots, as well as related transport locations, including freight-hauling train robbery shipments at off-load sites. Crimes vary depending on the availability and opportunity to "take goods" from a perceived weak display by law enforcement.

This uptick in opportunists' crime grew in locations where criminals perceived police indiscretions as alleged that followed the riots of 2020. Such places have become a magnet for organizations antagonistic to the rule of law, to local police, and to businesses. Unfortunately, the aftermath of their discontent and "victimization rhetoric" has exacerbated criminal behavior and caused costly damage to communities. In most of those locales (I did not say all), the police have been stripped of their authority, defunded, and forced to retreat into "observation status." Criminal opportunists have no concern for the public good. Destruction of property and fear among citizens are what they leave behind.

In the extreme, opportunistic crime leads to assaults on both police and citizens. It's recorded as incidental, isolated occurrences, and, in some cases, murder. Many of these criminals are highly mobile, traveling from state to state to offer vocal dissent on a particular social issue. This even includes the right to use public lands for their own personal prcfit. Confrontations with authorities leave behind physical destruction and suffering. These criminals will continue their defiant acts and expand into more areas with their audacious crimes if they perceive they will not be arrested and held accountable. Too often, given public sentiment, opportunistic criminals, posing as concerned citizens, will receive a free pass to move on to greater crimes that will cost all of us money to pay for their destruction.

In a short time span, this widespread criminal wave has become more confrontational to law enforcement authorities and to the general public. Progressively, they show little concern or consciousness for judicial consequences or remorse for their victims. As criminals, they increase unprovoked assaults and robbery against the elderly. Crimes occur in public places once considered safe havens. We've heard recent talk and whispers about the exploitation of child sex trafficking on a large scale; yet traffickers seldom seem to face arrests and prosecution. This escalation of violence against victimless people, innocent children, kidnappings, and other criminal activity is slowly invoking a cry from citizens.

Further targeted assaults and hate crimes against the Jewish and Asian communities and people of faith are rising. However, you have to make a deep dive to find the truth about who initiates these attacks on religious or historical sites, as most news reports never discover which criminal groups work behind the scenes. These assaults are often organized via social media. Such crimes against society and historical structures to diminish our history feel unreal to watch. It is a moral and human character issue tied to organized criminal activity.

The Change of Our Moral Compass

What is particularly disturbing to me is the lack of news media response and the absence of government authorities to enforce or take action following significant anti-social events, even when resulting in murders. Have you heard about suspicious arson at several of the nation's food and meat processing plants? Who is behind such vile acts that affect our food and clean water resources? Do we believe there are only natural occurrences? Can we simply believe such people silently slip out in the dark of night, leaving no trace? That, obviously, is not what is going on! My research and experience indicated that these individuals did not act without direction from shadowy entities bent on destroying our infrastructure and way of life.

The Career Criminal That I Knew

Much of the crime I see now is not the same type of criminal activity or perpetrator I saw working in the streets and in the prison system. My experience with criminals is vast. I've had too many encounters with them on the streets, in jails, and in prisons, along with extensive interviews with countless confidential informants, to understand them, then and now. This merging of new types of criminals operates differently. Their ability to organize sow discontent and now use social media to their advantage. This discontent only opens new avenues for crime. New-type groups, though not yet classified as career criminals or validated as gangs, have simply branched out into opportunistic "grab and go," "smash and grab" crimes, and frauds tied to Internet IT technology. Rewards for these "loot and scoot" crimes are increasingly greater than was once the bank robbery with greater profits. They are viewed as less criminal and less pursued.

Most of the career criminals I dealt with committed a lifetime of criminal behavior. Their records provide evidence of numerous crimes, yet in my encounters and interviews, I do not recall interacting with anyone who would arbitrarily victimize the elderly, children, or an innocent citizen riding the bus or subway. Although, I am aware today we see an increase of these crimes occurring, the images I see in the news do not appear to be the same type of criminal I dealt with. I am not referring to those who have *deviant* sex convictions; they are in a different category. Those men are viewed in a different light by fellow inmates. Even in prison, their peers see them as outcasts.

Yes. Many I encountered were predatory, especially of their own ethnic group. I know they came mostly from predator-prey environments on the streets, jails, and prisons. They dealt with adversaries who were rivals capable of intimidation at levels equal to their own. Those offenders nevertheless lived by a code, an imaginary line they did not cross. I know this may seem contradictory to everything characterized about them, but they too understood maintaining their own kind of structure. They understood the rules of the group and the hierarchy on the streets or while incarcerated. I am not a betting man, but if I were, I would bet that many in prison today—the kind of criminals I believe I know—do not like what is taking place in our streets and communities. Many of them have families in the communities where a great deal of these criminal acts are occurring.

But there is a difference between a stand-up criminal and a rogue, willful person(s) who would shoot up a school or social event just to kill, seek revenge or attack an ethnic group. In the prison environment, the career criminal inmate quickly and decisively acts against those who violate the elderly, women, or children. They police themselves, and among them, there exists a code of conduct that is not to be broken. The inmates could very well be our fathers, brothers, sons, uncles, and friends—just some who ran afoul of the law. But once incarcerated, they do what they must to survive in the violent world of prison. A few of the career criminals I encountered have turned their lives around, thus confirming my assessment of their acquiring new life goals. There is always optimism that some will change at some point in their lives; we all hope for a second chance and redemption.

The Emerging Career Criminal Today

What I see happening today feels different. These new types of criminals and crimes indiscreetly against unsuspected citizens. Members of a religious group or push someone in front of trains. Such acts of violence and targets of aggression have no justification. Too many people feel open animosity toward those with different political viewpoints, religions, and cultural beliefs. We continue to witness criminal activities following patterns of expedient crime based on perceived social injustices. These opportunists make purposeful choices, but they lack true moral judgment. Many believe they are entitled to or owed the same rewards enjoyed by people who earned a living through personal fortitude, a work ethic, and obeying the law.

Some believe their equality agendas, ideologies, and policies to universally/fundamentally change America may eventually win over voters committed to a democratic union founded and grounded by a Constitution and Bill of Rights. Others just participate in "destruction" for the thrill of excitement. Regrettably, they will continue their activities if they are not held accountable. These opportunists are visible yet seemingly invincible. Who are they? Where did they come from? Why have they not been identified or held accountable? Their groups are men and women of mixed ethnic backgrounds who exhibit an overt disdain for authority, property, and proprietorship. They grew from an experimentally reformist public ideology, but one sponsored by advocates who remain in the shadows. Some of these advocates hold positions of governmental authority where they vote for this viewpoint. Others pour their wealth towards these causes. They interpret "violent crimes" as misdemeanor offenses, but what is the political agenda that supports their end game?

Crimes of theft, carjacking, assault, fraud, and store looting are viewed as misdemeanors. It appears as if far too many police and prosecutors are refraining from taking action. Be assured, victims of these crimes are no less traumatized. The economic impact is immediate. Stores in neighborhoods are often victimized; many are closing, and corporate-owned businesses are moving to safer locations. How many small

grocery and drug stores have left troubled neigh-
bors in our city? How do these empty stores of goods
needed have an impact on citizens who now must use
public transportation and go elsewhere? Such criminal behavior has not abated and seems to be happening with more frequency into 2024.

Further, these acts of wholesale theft, "smash-
and-grab robberies, riotous behavior, and associated
destruction are perpetrated by groups of two or more
insular individuals disguising themselves with masks,
hoodies. Many do not appear to be spontaneous in
action, but more deliberate and organized. It is difficult to determine how organized this trend is or who
has sanctioned the activities. Who sells the stolen
property? Who plans the locations for the attacks?
Among the few individuals caught, many are young;
they lack extensive criminal backgrounds. Not all of
these offenders come from poverty-stricken backgrounds. Most are not the "state-raised" products of
the juvenile penal system. They appear less hardcore,
but each lacks a moral code for respecting the law,
and lawlessness. The range of ages varies from pre-
teen offenders to middle-aged adults. A distinctive difference from my previous career criminal profile is the
level of education many of these offenders may hold.
Some are college graduates, even holding advanced
degrees.

The opportunists excel at using slogans, rhetoric,
intimidation, and printing derisive speech online to
justify their acts. These openly anti-social actors are
organized; they act with purpose. If their crimes are
left unchallenged, they will continue to pursue criminal acts as they gain bravado. Many persons seen

committing crimes of opportunity in the summer of 2020 to present that I refer to are less likely to be identified as gang members or gang-related activity. Many come from and live in the suburbs. I would like to know their place of residence, financial means, the schools they attend, and the types of vehicles they own. It may surprise you to learn that these individuals may be involved in other types of criminal activities that are yet unknown. Citizens from all walks of life are asking questions like, "Why is it not a criminal justice priority to stop what appears to be a crime of opportunity?" I don't see things changing in the near future unless citizens take action against this attack on our communities. We must vote for individuals who stand for the rule of law.

CHAPTER 9
THE MEXICAN CARTELS-GROUP TWO:
The Supreme Opportunists

Mexican cartels, or Drug Trafficking Organizations, or DTOs, are the second category of criminals who do produce the most alarming threats to our communities. Operatives ascend out of Mexico and South/Central America, but predominantly Mexico. Their clients, who work for them and control various criminal enterprises, live and operate in nice neighborhoods in the United States. Their stronghold is along the United States border from leaders, "jefes" (bosses), who remain in Mexico calling the shots. Their prominence and destructive influence cannot be separated from the current immigration/border controversy and national immigration policy. Primarily, my initial focus was not on what is debated among political opponents or economic strategists about how to manage immigration. My center of attention is not political.

To add upon our national distress, since October, 2023 it has been hard to ignore the disturbing events and conflict taking place in Israel, the Gaza Strip, and Hamas. Nations and cultures are divided. Stability within the US and worldwide is shaken. Expressions of hatred and violence reinforce the vulnerability of bad actors—insurrectionists and terrorists—slipping through the US-Mexican border with bad intentions. May it not be another 9/11 lesson learned within the US.

At minimum, this message has another consequence: the unprecedented scale of illegal crossings by many, many thousands of single men from a myriad of foreign countries, neither unknown nor fully vetted. Haphazardly dispersed throughout the US is troublesome! In the near future, many will find themselves without work, financial means, or legal papers. Inactivity will lead to desperation for necessities. Those needing the necessities to survive will resort to criminal activity as a means to survive. Too often, together with substance abuse and excessive drinking, many of these men may commit crimes in a community. They will, if not already, also become opportunists for a broken system. Regrettably, I fear the worst is yet to come—a crime wave is in the making.

From the onset, my main focus and concerns is with the supreme opportunists, the Mexican cartels that control areas where new immigrants live; near and far from the border, cartels reign supreme. Their criminal reach and foothold within the US are tremendous and out of public scrutiny. They now have established a sophisticated system for illegal border crossers and many others to serve as "mules" for drug and sex trafficking and engage in other crimes of opportunity.

Mexican cartels' criminal activities are coordinated by leaders who reside in salacious ranches and elite neighborhoods in Mexico or elsewhere. We citizens suffer the aftermath of what they bring to our land. They have become the most widespread and prolific criminal enterprise of our time. Bigger than traditional organized crime of the 1920s Mafia up through the decades of prison gangs or other home-grown law-lessness groups. These supreme opportunists are cruel profiteers who shamefully exploit the system and dismay the immigration controversy. These Supreme opportunists are making unaccountable money by importing human cargo and illicit drugs, particu-larly fentanyl. This poison has the highest recorded drug-related death rate in history. The Cartels are the procurers of destruction responsible for the following:

- importation of people from multiple countries by way of total control of pas-sage through Mexico into the United States;
- generating unknown, but staggering prof-its;
- importation of unaccountable parentless children, ripe for child sexual slave labor exploitation;
- organized importation of narco-workers from Mexico and Latin America, special-ized employees trained and organized to integrate into established Cartel orga-nizations to transport items within the United States.

Their tentacles reach every urban and rural US region through drug distribution. The Cartels organize, con-trol, and enforce all illegal activities, and as smart busi-nessmen, they intend to build on their organizational proficiency and profit margins as follows:

- the Importation, transportation, taxation, and extortion of massive numbers of people passing from Mexico into many different ports of entry, their true identity, background, and intentions unknown to the United States. They don't care if "saboteurs" from other countries with bad intentions are among them;
- illegal exportation of stolen US vehicles to Mexico used at the pleasure of Mexican Cartels and wealthy citizens;
- importation of young individuals from Mexico and Central America who come illegally and then later entrench themselves in established violent street gangs. As major distributors of drugs for the Cartels, these youths account for much of the vicious crime long before the border crisis and will surely increase with new members;
- their known alliance with domestic and far-reaching California/Federal Mexican Mafia, who coordinate with Cartels and Latino Street gangs to distribute drugs across communities: a formal trifecta of drug distributors;
- exportation of weapons, often stolen or illegally purchased, then funneled into Mexico to terrorize citizens and government officials;
- exportation of millions, perhaps billions of untaxed monies gained illegally leaving the US for Mexico.

Such powerful criminal organizations appear to function with impunity; they survive behind battlefield fortifications operating near the United States/Mexican border. This *should be* more disturbing to those willing to sanction millions of illegal immigrants who cross the border saying they need asylum from abusive governments.

Among themselves, Mexican cartels in the US compete to control the drug distribution market. Drugs are distributed to regional street gangs that answer to a cartel. Street gang members work on a short profit margin. They are not Cartel members per se, but they are accountable to precisely reimburse the Cartels when payment is due.

Mexican cartels are involved in the entire drug apparatus, from the importation of chemicals from China to the transporter, manufacturer, distributor, and user. They have their own Cradle to Grave process: they will lie, cheat, steal, rob, mug, assault, prostitute others, and disturbingly even commit murder to get drugs to market. At the user level, they depend on drug addiction to complete the circle for prof t.

At the distribution level, Cartels utilize specialized runners and transporters responsible for delivering tax and profit back to Mexico. Brokers controlled by higher-level intermediary's tax every level; it is true that every player gets a cut of the profits, but the Cartels get the lion's share. It is a vast pyramid directed and coordinated through our Southwestern states, one that extends internationally.

Specialized real estate brokers purchase, manage, sell, and rent residential and commercial property to launder money and turn it into profit. Many are used for stash houses to store their drugs and some for party houses. They have shown up in localities in remote, isolated areas to grow their own brand of marijuana. They utilize paid associates who specialize in the complexities of filing and recording property deeds. Some are legit filings, and some are frauds. On the outskirts of many rural towns near the border with Mexico, police are often called to monitor modern mansions, safely hidden inside high cement walls, some with sophisticated technical surveillance equipment. These are the "elder generation homes" for family members living in the US. They offer protection and safety to Cartel members, family, and close associates.

For some time, Cartels has used construction companies to build commercial and residential properties in Mexico and the US. Many of these US companies have no idea who is funding the projects as they are layered through un-scrutinized banking and cut-outs of unidentified individuals. Have you noticed the fabulous resorts on both the coasts of Mexico and Baja California, Mexico? Do you feel safe vacationing there, at least till now? Clients and Cartel associates buy, finance, and manage commercial enterprises such as restaurants, nightclubs, laundromats, money loan exchanges, and countless other establishments that can launder illegally transferred funds. Initially, they were located in predominantly Hispanic and Latino neighborhoods, but now many have moved to suburbia. We can thank the Cartels for their generosity in delivering imported foods, entertainment, and other amenities we enjoy. Should we not be concerned about the "who" profits behind these entertainment establishments?

Cartel *associate* clientele also specializes in the purchase of weapons, legal and illegal. Their equipment matches that of our police and, in many cases, even the military. I wonder just how many gun store burglaries throughout the US are attributed to cartels. Over the last two decades in Arizona, police have responded (after the fact) to numerous burglaries of gun shops. Great quantities of every weapon category left these businesses. Where did they go? Who are the suspects? Why have none been arrested? Don't believe the simplistic answer; they are not being sold at gun shows. The Cartels are moving them out of the US.

Yes, cartels are organized, powerful, and ruthless, and they enjoy unlimited financial resources, given our current social trend toward more lenient punishments. Cartels are experiencing newfound unlimited profits from an inviting international flow of immigrants to the US. Some are sent on to Canada and other nations. The Cartels have emissaries and networks that interface with countries worldwide. Given the number of different ethnic groups the US Border Patrol identifies from across the globe, we see that cooperation exists internationally. I say again, too many have been identified as coming from countries opposed to a democratic America, even hostile to our way of life. Even more disturbing is the many who have been identified on the terrorist watch list. I ask, what are their intentions?

But something more disturbing is the fact that Mexico's government is no longer simply challenged by one or two and even three cartels. The Mexican government is now confronted by at least seven significant cartels that mirror small armies. The cartels also control independent criminal organizations within Mexico. Elected officials fear crossing these powerful forces. My research shows Cartels are attempting to control Mexico's fisheries and coastal ports. In addition, they have confronted the federal gas and oil industry with truck carjacking and threats to anyone reporting these crimes.

I have gained much insight into the potential harm that having a narco-terrorist state as our neighbor can bring to the US. Should the US government demand more from the Mexican government in confronting and controlling this threat to our safety and to the economy? I know this subject is hard to discuss. I do know the Cartels had members in prisons and jails during my time identifying and profiling career criminals and have forged new criminal associates. They will continue to inflict casualties and destruction across the United States, if not impeded, and reign supreme as opportunists.

CHAPTER 10
TOOLS OF THE TRADE
The Interviews

There was no better way to find out what was happening than to go to the primary source for answers. I knew the importance of first-hand information, so I began a campaign to interview inmates in county jails and prisons. Initially, the process was more based on instinct than following a predetermined method. I began to identify and seek out gang leaders of all races and other non-affiliated high-profile inmates. I looked for those with extensive criminal histories. I learned the importance of initially speaking with the staff classification counselors at the facilities. They had informative background information about the inmate, and they were willing to share.

All county, state, and federal correctional facilities maintain an inmate data file system. When available, I reviewed an inmate's file, which, in prison slang, is referred to as their jacket. These files, mostly automated today, contained a wealth of information, including criminal history, pre-sentence reports, family background, edu-

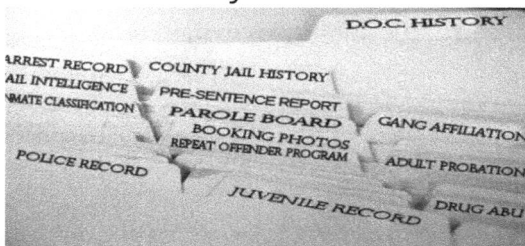

cation and work history, mental and physical health, psychological evaluations, and other good-to-know details about their backgrounds. I wrote on yellow-lined notepads or three-ring, red memory-finding journals in my first few years. I took extensive notes daily, documenting the chronological events in the subject's life before the interview. Today, such files are mostly automated; but, to me, having a file in my hands and looking for a nugget of information was like following a treasure map.

During those interviews, I had notes to ask questions about the chronological events in the subject's life. These simple yellow notepads and journals served as research documents, a great tool that allowed me to dig deep into a subject's background. I later used the records I developed and turned them into dossiers for identifying and validating prison gang members. Over the years, these dossiers proved invaluable while conducting investigations, developing intelligence reports, cultivating sources, or assisting other agencies with their investigations. Inevitably, when I raised questions of a personal nature, the interviewees were taken aback by how much I knew about them, especially during a first-time interview with a cop many knew nothing about.

I never revealed to them how I knew this information. This approach was the best method to maintain control during the interview. I continuously overwhelmed them with questions concerning their past. It also required me not to settle for a cursory response to a question. I noticed that if I was disciplined and persistent enough during an interview, they were reluctant to lie for fear of being caught, or worse, something revealed in their past they did not want exposed to their peers. They sometimes tried to lie to me, but usually only once. These types of rather non-threatening interviews differ from those conducted after apprehending a suspect when seeking a confession.

I also conducted interviews in creative places with suspects of different races, backgrounds, and personalities—often right on the streets, in my duty car, at restaurants, or wherever arrangements could be made. I was assisted many times by other justice personnel who introduced me to their sources. These exchanges provided me with the framework of material I later taught. They consisted of my observations and analysis of identifiable profile traits and shared beliefs. But most important, I had first-hand data from the subject's own telling.

During these encounters, either on the streets or in jails or prisons most of the subjects were initially cautious. They were self-assured, assertive, and very persuasive. A few tried to intimidate me. I normally remained low-key with a calm voice but was straight-forward; however, if threatened with overt intimidation, I assumed a new persona to match their assertiveness. It would have been a momentous mistake to allow them to bulldog or intimidate me, so I held my ground. To not stand firm would be perceived as a fatal weakness. There are few secrets in prisons, and the word gets around about an inmate's influence. I had to meet that if I hoped to gain information.

An antagonistic response was particularly prominent from a few members of the Arizona AB. In hindsight, I've wondered if it may have arisen from my lineage being Anglo-Hispanic and my carrying the moniker of "Paco." But I came to realize that in their world, it really doesn't matter what your race, religion, gender, or size is. It's how you carry yourself and come across that matters most. No one asked me about my family background, nor would I say; but; in the end, I successfully interfaced with many imprisoned Aryan Brotherhood members.

The Arizona prison system had two Hispanic prison gang factions at the time, competing for the title of the Arizona Mexican Mafia. We referred to them as the "New" and "Old " Mexican Mafias to distinguish the two groups. There was also the Aryan Brotherhood and a black inmate faction known as the Mau Maus. Arizona did not have the Black Guerrilla Faction that was in California. By the mid 1980s, the Border Brothers of Mexican Nationals and the Sureños were becoming dominant players in the Arizona DOC. Today, many state prison systems populations are made up of individuals who came from elsewhere and migrated to their state in pursuance of crime opportunities and to increase numbers of an established gang. So, by showing knowledge during these types of interviews—their family background, where they came from and prior criminal history—in a calm, deliberate manner with inmates outside of Arizona will serve you well as an interview tool.

The Unexpected Schooling
Another successful interview tool I acquired came about mostly out of distress, came close to the beginning of my prison gang assignment ; and I used it many times afterward. I asked prisoners to "school"

me on things in "their world." This approach, coupled with showing them respect when deserved and being a good listener, allowed them to tell their story while providing me with up-to-date information. I stumbled across this "schooling" technique in my first interview with a fierce, well-known, validated California Mexican Mafia member living in Phoenix, Arizona named "Mandi". My introduction came through a fellow narcotics detective. Upon our introduction, this man looked at me with chilling eyes, as defiant as any bad guy I had ever encountered. He asked, "What do you want from me *ese*?" (Guy or dude in Spanish) That question was so direct it caught me off-guard. There was a brief period of silence.

To this day, I don't know how it occurred to me to say, "I need some schooling." He paused, looked at me, smiled, and said, "Schooling . . . I like that." I met him at various times afterward and learned a great deal about his history with the California Mexican Mafia. Because of his circumstances in California, whenever I met with him on the streets or in restaurants, he was always guarded by the surroundings and armed with a knife.

I had not seen him for several months; then one day I was notified by a DPS dispatcher that the county hospital had a patient who wanted to see me. It was Mandi. The next day I went to his hospital room where he was hooked up to IV tubes and had lost so much weight that I hardly recognized him. He told me he had to check into the hospital. I'm sure his condition was due to his heroin use. He was not fully coherent when he asked me to open the drawer of a small table next to his hospital bed. Inside was a folded piece of paper, and as I opened it, he said, "That's the name and telephone number of my ex-old lady. Paco, she transcribed or wrote a couple hundred pages of my life; she knows everything. You tell the 'bitch' that I said to give it to you."

I knew I could not tell her what he said, but I called her and asked if she could give me a copy of historical data. She said no; she was planning to get it published. She wanted to meet at a bar to talk it over, but I felt uncomfortable, so I never heard from her again. I wished she had published it. Mandi was a very interesting and dangerous dude, so it probably would have been a very informative, eye-opening book. Mandi became a lasting contact up to his death. His last few words were, "Paco, I'm in the box. It's my turn." He passed away a short time afterwards I visited with him.

The Unwilling Opponent
There were those few I encountered who had such distrust for authority that, when approached, they completely shut down. They would give me no time. These convicts told me, "You got nothing coming," all the while sizing me up; in those cases, I knew there was no need to proceed. To be fair, not all criminal inmates displayed such overt animosity. Some enjoy talking, especially those seasoned by years of incarceration. They were familiar with how the criminal justice "system" works.

They know how to play the game; they understand the interview is in their best interest, so they should show respect. Conversely, pushback also comes from some I least expect. The old saying "nothing personal, just business" comes to mind. The prison interview process is not for the faint of heart or for anyone who can't take rejection. Some inmates are willing to talk as a countermeasure. They want to discover who you are, what you are after, and how much you know. So, obviously, we had concerns about these prison gang members—the Aryan Brotherhood and Mexican Mafia members—knowing they could command someone on the outside to find out our personal information. My vast number of prison interviews resulted in a few individuals becoming long-term sources of information; I built up respect and trust with them. Letting a man talk and not giving away information is a lesson that takes a while to develop.

The Face-To-Face Encounter: A Showdown
Working with career criminals can be challenging. An example of how fiction comes close to reality was depicted in a scene from my favorite movie, *Heat*, starring Al Pacino and Robert De Niro, and directed by Michael Manning. The movie's theme centers on a squad from the Los Angeles Police Department's elite robbery/homicide division led by a profound and obsessive Lieutenant Hanna (Pacino). He is targeting a group of career criminals headed by their foremost leader, McCauley (De Niro).

The film's characters show what I describe about the career criminal's profile. The movie implies that all characters and associates with McCauley's robbery crew are ex-convicts who had served prison time together or were referred to McCauley by other close criminal associates as "stand-up" guys—men who could be trusted. The thought of going back to prison did not deter them. They were career criminals. They were willing to risk hitting this bank in the daytime in downtown Los Angeles. They were going for the big score with a predetermined willingness to confront the police if apprehended. They knew they were being watched but thought they could outsmart their police adversaries.

The film reveals the real psychology and antisocial personality of many career criminals. During surveillance by the robbery/homicide squad to take down McCauley's crew, two main antagonists, Lieutenant Hanna and McCauley, oddly grow to share a mutual respect for one another. Both were at the top of their game, anticipating a day ending with a confrontation during a takedown. Every major career criminal involved in long-term criminal activity knows that day will come, but that does not deter them. They are serious about what they do using their successful techniques.

This criminal mindset was portrayed vividly in the scene at the dinner where Hanna and McCauley impulsively meet over a cup of coffee at a diner. They begin discussing what fate lay ahead for them should a confrontation follow the attempted bank robbery. The scene was surreal; those who have talked with criminals know what I mean. Taking this caricature into the real world, Lieutenant Hanna didn't respect McCauley as you would a brother, peer, or mentor. Instead, he respected McCauley as a tactician—for his intuitiveness, his attention to detail, and as an adversary.

Of all my encounters with career criminals, there are only a few to whom I would give such accolades. One is still in the game and will probably never change, even in old age. Others walked away from crime; they simply got tired of being locked down. A few others were resurrected through their relationship with the Lord. I have witnessed their lives since their redemption, so I know how they live today.

Do not be mistaken in thinking a majority of career criminals lack intelligence or come from poverty. Many I know have high IQ scores. They were informative and knowledgeable on many subjects. However, most did lack a higher education or degree. Perhaps they did not have the discipline required to spend years studying textbooks and listening to lectures. Many came from environments where education is not a priority or is seemingly out of reach. They possessed skill sets that furthered their criminal lives instead of the skill sets society applauds. Had they applied the skills they exhibited in socially approved jobs within social norms, their lives might have led to unlimited success.

This is especially true for those who have committed their lives to organized criminal groups and displayed leadership. These "Shot callers" possess executive skills, shrewdness, and engaging attributes. For some, this includes ruthlessness. These characteristics place them at the top of an organization respected among their peers. They are the innovators in persuasion—men directing criminal activity with followers working the streets or plotting revenge and retribution.

A Case in Point: Joe Bonanno

In 1979, my long-time, loyal friend and partner, Agent Bill Richardson, and I played a small role in the investigation of mafia boss Joseph "Joe" Bonanno in Tucson,

Arizona. In later years, Bill became a top-notch sex crimes detective with the Mesa Police Department. Joe was the founding boss of one of five New York organized crime organizations. But at this time in his long career, he had been exiled to Tucson, due to internal misgivings among the crime families. The investigation was for a conspiracy to endeavor to obstruct justice; it was initiated by the Federal Bureau of Investigation (FBI) and the ADCD Narcotics Strike Force, for which Bill and I worked. We were assigned to the day-shift surveillance team along with four FBI agents brought in from other duty locations across the United States to assist in the investigation.

Joe became a mafia boss by possessing leadership skills and personality attributes similar to those of a respected corporate president. He established his credentials from past work he had accomplished. He had worked up to this position since his youth. Like a corporate manager, Joe climbed the ladder to head a mafia family named after him, the Bonanno Organized Crime Family. Joe was alleged to be using pay phones throughout Tucson to conduct business in other states as well as in Canada. Surveillance was essential to record when Joe made these phone calls. Two of Joe's trusted mafia family members came to Tucson with him, ostensibly as bodyguards. They drove him to the pay phones. From the beginning, we knew we were in the company of professionals.

Throughout the weeks of surveillance, they used every trick in the book to evade surveillance. I was lucky to be part of our team, as there is no better way to improve counter-surveillance skills than advanced on-the-job training by the original mobsters. I could picture them during their younger days on the streets of New York, evading the New York Police Department, the FBI, and their criminal rivals, busting red lights, executing quick left turns, and all the other tactics in their playbooks to avoid surveillance that their success required.

Like Joe, a slight few fall under the category of professional, experienced career criminals, meaning men who worked years to master "crime as a way of life." Crime sustained Joe personally and economically. He developed a cadre of enterprises. Based on his outward appearance, social status, and influence, we have to say Joe was a successful businessman. He portrayed a legitimate image. Joe had avoided what lesser career criminals experience—arrests, convictions, incarcerations, and often a life sentence. The majority of criminals follow this path throughout their history; there are few exceptions, like Mr. Bonanno.

Joe is an example of a career criminal who could successfully control any organized group. But Joe's type is a special exception to the norm. He was insulated and difficult to pursue. During that stage in his career, I sensed I was witnessing someone unique. In his forty-year involvement with the mafia, Joe had never gone to prison, and, to my knowledge, he did not have a felony arrest. In his late sixties, he was spry, energetic, and he carried himself with a regal aura. He was alert to his surroundings, and we knew he was watching for us.

The Watchful Eye

I discovered another technique useful during my visits to the prison. When I could, I watched inmate behavior from a surveillance location so I could note individual mannerisms and interactions with their peers. I looked for characteristics I could identify if I saw them on the streets later. This pre-interview data collection revealed who had influence and who the true leaders were. I knew if they conducted themselves in this manner while incarcerated, they would continue to do so upon release. For several years as a detective with the Arizona Department of Public Safety, these observations proved invaluable in assisting other police department robbery detectives in Maricopa County. From time to time, I reviewed videotape captured during armed robberies (with detectives from the Phoenix, Mesa, and Scottsdale Police Departments). My earlier observations helped solve a few of these cases.

On one occasion, while reviewing the video of a robbery with a dogged and highly successful Scottsdale Police Robbery detective, Tom Van Metter, I spotted who I thought was an Aryan Brotherhood member. Although his face was partially concealed, he could not hide his body language. I was familiar with his mannerisms, having noted his unique physical characteristics in prior surveillance, and I was able to identify him. Unquestionably, the many dozens of interviews and observations over many years helped with investigations and solved crimes.

I recommend officers assigned to work robberies, either the FBI or local police, team up with prison investigators from their jurisdiction. I recommend they reach out to these investigators and utilize their knowledge of inmates released to the streets. They will likely see their unsolved robberies go down. By noting how some inmates simply stand out, whether in an incarcerated population or on the street, I came to understand that those men demand your recognition and attention. Their ultimate goal is to gain power once released from prison, which starts with control over others through intimidation for personal profit, and crime robbery is one way to get it.

CHAPTER 11
THE REQUIRED LEARNING

Law enforcement officers pursuing career criminals within their jurisdiction should know who they are, where they reside, and what their violence potential is after release. This is why liaison contacts with law enforcement within the parole or probation division, the Department of Corrections, and county jail facilities are important before an inmate is released. Officers can review what is contained within the subject's prison or jail institutional file to identify multiple criminal activities, such as illegal weapons possession, assaults, narcotics, armed robbery, sex crimes, burglary, etc. Are they spontaneous or methodical in their activities? Do they commit crimes alone or with a crew? Look for associates and relatives. This is the time to familiarize yourselves with those who are coming or in the community.

This same profile information applies to the most violent Outlaw Motorcycle Gangs (OMG), extremist groups, cartel members, and terrorists. It is the career criminal's mindset, bad intentions, and experience that set him apart from other less committed members. This is especially important in the pre-planning stages before placing undercover officers in known threat groups. Did the backup unit task someone to study the assignments to identify members within the group who pose the greatest risk to officers?

This pre-planned work-up also applies to the execution of search and arrest warrants while in spontaneous situations—responding to live shooting incidents, armed encounters in progress, crimes of violence, or the use of a weapon—information on a subject's background will likely not be available. Responding personnel should understand they will encounter those with a predetermined mindset to use violence against them. We must become students of their mindset, traits, and characteristics to control the situation. Additionally, we must learn how and where to obtain information and communicate our findings from correctional settings to law enforcement officers working the streets. We need to inform all officers for their safety and that of the community.

As I gained experience, I began to question why there was no specialized training concerning this type of experienced criminal—data vital to the protection of patrol officers working in dangerous neighborhoods. Every patrol officer deserves to know which criminals in the area are most likely to violently confront him or her. At a minimum, bank employees and convenience store clerks should be informed of the "give-away mannerism" a robber may usually exhibit just prior to the robbery occurring.

These few seconds may provide time to take an evasive or alternative measure. This is training that deserves further consideration. I also questioned why this subject is not addressed on a national level by top police and federal agency officials, including national coverage by the news media. As crime destroys our cities and towns, I am asking these same questions today.

One technique we used on very few occasions was carefully thought-out messaging utilizing misinformation or disinformation; spoken messages were carefully considered and purposefully inserted to raise interest. We hoped the message would reach other non-affiliated inmates and produce sources. It was, is, a tool to be used when rumors of something imminent are to happen. In our case, an example would be to intervene when a potential riot or gain knowledge of a murder being plotted. We could think up something of controversy this way to our advantage, both during interviews and in casual conversation. We anticipated a "disinformation message" would get back to gang members and circulate. It could solicit a response that would come our way. We wanted to plant a seed that suggested we were "in-the-know." We wanted them to think we already knew everything they had planned. Such a message could confirm or deny the internal rumors we were hearing. Our goal was to keep the inmates off balance and rouse internal suspicion. We wanted to evoke sources who could reveal their plans so we could design countermeasures.

Don't think this technique is not still used, even in our troubling times. Media outlets, political parties, big business, and governmental agencies, at home and abroad, employ "suspicious, speculative messages," some close to the truth and others purposely misleading. Big Tech uses misrepresented facts as "evidence." This misuse of "truth to power" has tainted a legitimate intelligence tool. "Near-truth" or "suspected facts" can be useful to fact-check an inmate's response and sub-stantiate or flesh out information someone "hinted at." It helps interviewers get leads not ordinarily avail-able by other means. As I knew then, we were on the outside looking in, so we needed to use every tool at our command to learn what they were up to. In keep-ing with safety and security, be it a prison or national concerns, we are always on the outside looking in.

CONCLUSION
The Crime Story Now and Future

Universally, the study of crime, punishment, and incarceration within the United States is unique. In comparison to many other nations with political influence, the US remains a nation that extols free speech, even hate speech that may conflict with a myriad of social agendas. In jails and prisons, we also provide unprecedented rights to offenders. Generally, prisons and jails in the United States, when compared to most other nations, are unmatched in benefits. The goal is to provide safety, shelter, nutrition, and medical treatment for all inmates.

Further, we consider alternative programs such as probation, community work release programs, counseling, and drug treatment services, mainly paid for by state governments. Logic suggests individuals who live in such a nation as ours, free from tyranny, enjoying respect for individual rights, unparalleled employment, education, social benefits, and health services, would cherish freedom above all else. Yet, the United States is designated as having the largest incarceration rate of any nation. Seemingly, it is contradictory. Why?

Conversely, prisons and jails can be dangerous places where evil intentions grow. It is a playground for the predatory minds. It does not matter what level of prison an inmate starts in; even a low-level, soft prison, mistakenly called the "Country Club" prison, can teach a young man new criminal tactics. The Level I prison is touted as having an atmosphere free from violent offenders and gang influences. Do not be fooled; that is a myth. The crime of an offender and prison location do not always depict the nature and mindset of an individual who stays there, especially one who wants trouble. This predatory type of individual exists in all prison and jail environments. Though they may be housed in a maximum-security prison or the lowest classification of incarceration, they exist everywhere.

Multiple disciplines have researched the causes of crime and incarceration in America. The emphasis as cited emphasizes poverty, drug addiction, physical and mental abuse, absentee fathers, gang influence, homelessness and, of late, matters of equity. All are important symptoms. There is little doubt that certain segments of the population feel the helplessness of poverty and social deprivation. Desperate people often take desperate measures to free themselves from base circumstances. Despair (economic or emotional) may override concern for consequences, resulting in acting on impulse with little forethought of consequences. In some inmate cases, incarceration may be a better alternative to saving the person's life or the lives of others. Youths growing up in neighborhoods with a strong anti-police and/or gang culture often use crime as a prestige status and reward system. They learn this and carry the idea into prison. Incarceration just increases this power. After release, as ex-inmates, they "return to the hood" and old behaviors. On the contrary, there are untold examples of individuals from such environments who never run afoul of the law and become successful and productive citizens.

I deduce that many studies with theory and analysis concerning crime are researched by academics who have spent minimal time inside a prison or jail setting. Most crime statistics used in such studies are taken from the Federal Bureau of Investigations (FBI) reports submitted annually by state and local criminal justice entities. Additional research is conducted and transmitted via universities on federal grants to support a multi-cause sociological theory.

These paths ultimately land in the hands of policymakers. However, social theories seldom touch on the criminal's mindset, his ways of making choices, his understanding of free will, and his definition of morality. Few explore the "why" of an individual's choice as he pursues a life of growing criminal behavior. This pattern of learned behavior may start with a seemingly insignificant criminal act (stealing beer from Circle K on Saturday night), but with increasing boldness and audacity, the youth learns the ways of the career criminal. He enters a way of life outside of social and community norms. He is free of the American work ethic. He learns how and where he can seize easy money by "just taking" what he can for personal profit.

Much of my law enforcement and correction career has been spent on the streets or working inside prisons and jails. While traveling across the United States attending conferences, I attempted to visit the local jail or prison. Each occasion was enlightening. I explored and asked questions about the makeup of the inmate population in terms of race and ethnicity, and I always asked, "What impact do gang members have within the facility? What kinds of crimes were common in the inmate population? Which inmates were problematic, and why?"

Because much of what I have related I gleaned while conducting inmate interviews. I approached the interviews purposefully, always seeking to discover the person's personal and criminal background, beliefs, and motivations. These questions can be answered in simple conversations.

I am convinced that a high percentage of incarcerated inmates in the US today is made up largely of individuals with a career criminal mindset; most are purposely working their way to that status. Committing criminal acts is a choice. Every career criminal I encountered acknowledged that he moved along a criminal path by choice, not by coercion. It is not, as often said, the majority of individuals who are downtrodden or impoverished that fall into this category. True, many come from poverty, but many also from the affluent-upper and middle-class neighborhoods also make that choice.

Regrettably, our correctional facilities have all too often taken the place of mental health facilities. Prison is not the place for those with severe mental disorders. These individuals require services beyond the capacity and resources of most correctional organizations. The requirements and strain on staff for these special prisoners deplete resources that could be used for meaningful rehabilitation programs. Those inmates with paranoid psychopathic disorders can be a threat to other inmates as well. Patients with lingering mental conditions are not adequately treated in prison.

When released from correctional confinement, they account for a large portion of homeless shelters and street camps, with men found lingering in parks or back alleys. Those afflicted with paranoia and schizophrenia are seen wielding a machete or pushing someone in the path of a train. The number of mentally ill ex-convicts is growing nationally, and with excessive drug use and alcoholism, their crimes harm innocent citizens. This is a problem state legislators should address as they work with administrators of jails and prisons as well as with forensic behaviorists. Many mentally ill ex-prisoners should not be released directly to the community. Perhaps it's time we re-assess, bringing back mental hospitals better equipped to provide professional care and evaluation. There is a need to prioritize and set a national agenda on societal ills if we are to remain a nation whereas others chose to come.

The New Officer-Involved Shootings and Mass Casualties

Today's patrol officers work at great risk. Criminals have lost their fear of confrontation and its consequences. Police are in the sights of criminal hunters, just as one would stalk a deer. Extremists who choose a path of crime are usually acting on some skewed ideology or a mental disorder and come from all walks of life and social backgrounds. As I take notice of officer-involved shootings, I'm interested in the offender's history. Did the officer engaged in a shooting incident have a chance to question the subject for his mental outlook and criminal history? Of course not.

An officer working the streets has no way to know if any psychological evaluation of the criminal he faces has been fully vetted. Was this person just released from incarceration? How can an officer stopping an impaired driver or someone involved in domestic trouble know if he is a patient under psychological care for prior violent incidents? It is clear, universally, that no national pathway exists for disseminating this type of preventive information to officers working the streets in any community.

The multi-targeted shootings and mass casualty's situations call for a new type of alert system as an extension to the 911 system, which dispatch centers have access to for immediate referral and is standardized on a national level. The 911 emergency call may be all a citizen victim knows to use. But this method of asking for help has become too all-encompassing—a catch-all used to report a barking dog, clear up to suicide prevention, and domestic disputes. It is ingrained in our society and should be left in place. Its original application, by itself, did not consider nor plan for mass casualties and tragic events that would later happen in the US.

In many locations throughout the US, the local 911 operators may lack both training and resources in their area to resolve present, imminent, or impending mass casualties and threat situations, such as 9/11, on their own through our current use of 911. Such incidents now require on-the-spot communication of a higher nature with specialized, trained police or government organizations outside and in addition to their local jurisdiction.

This has obviously been shown by scrutinizing past events, rather than a call for more manpower than a responding officer or two can provide or even a local SWAT team. Especially in rural or smaller departments, responding to critical and potential mass casualty situations requires additional specialized resources and personnel to respond immediately and are located in close proximity to the situation. The rise in catastrophes, most often involving mass casualties, shootings, and terrorist threats, requires a national, regional, and coordinated effort with expedient resources that we currently do not have in place at the level that it may call for.

Such a platform may already exist through the Regional Information Sharing System (RISS) program. RISS comprises six regional project locations throughout the US. Each project links law enforcement agencies from neighboring states into a regional network that interacts with law enforcement member agencies nation-wide. RISS is funded by the United States Congress through the Bureau of Justice Assistance.

RISS is a secure national intelligence-based network offering a myriad of valuable resources ideally suited to expanding their current capabilities for a mass casualty central dispatch repository call out system.

Each of the six regional RISS projects, in conjunction and coordination with their member agencies

911 dispatch centers, then enables expedited pass-through access to a 24-hour selected response team assigned in stand-by mode by RISS agency members with standby airmobile access. If not with RISS, then we must choose a program that meets these mandates. There is a feeling of expediency in the air. The points of view and opinions of this author concerning the RISS Network do not represent the official policies of the United States Department of Justice.

The Cold War Threat

Law enforcement is in a national cold war. Because officers lack foreknowledge of potential adversaries lurking in contact situations, they are increasingly the subject of scorn and ridicule if forced to use deadly force during an engagement with an uncontrollable, violent subject. In recent times, police have been used as fall-guys for political expediency and anti-police rhetoric. A clear dictionary definition of how "Cold War Threat" fits what the police are accused of not handling exists: It is "any condition of rivalry, mistrust, or open hostility short of violence, especially between power groups (such as labor or management), or confrontations between the parties' more liberal and more conservative members over America's involvement in social conflicts." These huge sociological debates lie outside the job description of a police officer.

The police are too often caught in the middle of issues unrelated to the enforcement of the law, such as responding to a political figure's demand for personal service or disputes over parental concerns during a school board meeting. These first-line field officers are required to do as they are told by their superiors. At the same time, crime and criminality are still pervasive in those communities.

My recent research makes this point clear: the same career criminal, the repetitive criminal, is responsible for crimes at all levels and subject to police focus. What we face now and in the future is the 'Resurrected Opportunist', a type of emerging criminal learning how to become a career criminal. The legal system in many cases is providing him with this opportunity.

These opportunists and expansionists are responsible for many of the violent encounters we have seen, heard, and read about. When you read about "a smash and grab" incident at a jewelry or clothing store, think "career criminal in the making." Right now, this connection is not fully publicized, scrutinized, or recognized. We are not told or warned about who the thieves are or what they represent as part of the larger criminal population. As I write, I have serious concerns for future or past elections results regardless of political affiliation. Are plans being made to target elections, resulting in civil disobedience and riots? Will our elected representatives understand the need to provide resources, and funds that give the police the added support necessary to control the potentially divisive forces operating in darkness? A more ominous, threatening concern exists for who we are as a nation. This moral question goes beyond the singular profile, human nature, and emphasis on the career of a criminal or gang.

The sudden epidemic of crime across America is real. It is not a mirage, nor should the problem be downplayed by the news media or a small percentage of activists on a national level with a political ideology of activism, rationalization, or a perception for social equality. The addition of more citizens' investigative committees alone will not stop the epidemic. Untrained citizens, even those with the best interests of the "common good," cannot solve these serious national and international crime problems. Although it is a worthy cause to pursue, it is a moral issue that each of us must take time to ponder to decide how and when we must speak out and to whom. A democracy depends on the will of the people. We are the people who must act if we care to preserve the way of life we enjoy.

ADDENDUM

The writing of my manuscript began around June 2022. I was in a very lonely, dark place, finding myself alone after the passing of my wife and companion of fifty years together in August 2022 with breast cancer that had so quickly spread to her lungs. Uncertainty and loneliness do strange things to your head. Evan, before the diagnoses, untold tests, lump removal surgery, chemotherapy, CAT scan results, closely followed oxygen, and eventual morphine and hospice assistance. Even before all that, I was deeply concerned by events unfolding in the US after the George Floyd incident in May 2020.

You don't spend over forty years of your life dedicated to fighting crime, serving your country in military service, and believing in law and order only to see it torn apart by riots, unabated destruction of historical sites, looting, arson, and direct attacks on law enforcement without feeling unbelief and anger. Especially by people dressed in mostly black attire with masks covering their faces.

To make matters worse in a short time span, a movement was sweeping the nation with defunding the police and the implementation of measures restricting the police from intervening while unyielding crime was taking place by people using the same means to hide their identity. The masking of America by COVID-19 has led to more unseen repercussions than ever anticipated.

Watching the news night after night of these events playing out. I began to question who these individuals

of observant mixed races are. Of different sophistica-
tion and degrees of violence. They seemed to spring
up from city to city—from state to state. To make matters worse, after the 2020 presidential election, our
former border policies were swept away, allowing for
historic mass illegal aliens into the US unchecked and
unvetted. Many, many from countries outside of the
US, and the scariest of all, are untold on the terrorist
watch list. I *knew* what all this would lead to, which I
covered in the book you are now holding in your hand.
It was difficult to watch because, in the latter half of
my career, I was a student and eventual teacher of
criminal behavior, particularly career criminals.

Months prior to finishing my manuscript, and
for the last few months my book has been in the
care of my editor and now published. The writing of
these unanswered questions, which I gamely tried to
cover—the answers to who, what, when, where, and
why. Things are not getting better; they are getting
worse. The unexpected war between Israel and Hamas
has resulted in riots and the takeover of several universities and in our streets. The calling out of hatred
and destruction of Israel, Jews, Christians and other
choices of faith was never before witnessed within the
US and worldwide.

Like a self-fulfilling prophecy, the things I started
writing about in my book to come, are happening. We
are witnessing increasing crimes of rape and murder.
Fentanyl overdoses should shock our conscience. This
does not account for the impact on our economy of
mass migration, affecting all public and private medical and education services. Somehow, someway,
and soon, a change, a plan, and a new and immedi-

ate vision are needed—no requirement. There is no time for complacency. As a democratic nation, people have a choice to make at the ballot box. You will have to decide what kind of future you want to live in. The political arena has become derisive, nasty, and contemptible. It harms friendships and family relationships and tears apart the fabric of our nation; but, in spite of its consequences, I would rather choose to live in a democratic nation where I am free to make my own choice.

Last, on July 14, 2024, the attempted assassination of former President Trump in Pennsylvania. Then, on September 16, a second assassination was made at his Mar-a-Lago golf course in Florida. When 'rhetoric' is cited by some, it becomes a passive approval to harm, and this nation has lost its moral compass. What have we become? Like him or not, it must be a wake-up call to us all.

APPENDIX

If you are researching prior information on this subject matter, the following venues may assist you:

Google: Frank "Paco" Marcell or Frank Marcell Career Criminal

Publications:
[U.S. Department of Justice, Office of Justice Programs NCJ Number 200899

Career Criminals, Security Threat Groups and Prison Gangs: An Interrelated Threat. FBI Bulletin Volume: 72 Issue6 Dated: June 2003] David M Allender, Frank Marcell

[Police 1 Preparing to Confront & Control Career Criminals? by Charles Remberg interview with Frank Marcell, August 27, 2006-Part 1]

[Police 1 Are You Prepared to Win Against Today's Career Criminal? By Charles Remberg interview with Frank Marcell, August 23, 2006-Part 2]

IN MEMORIAM

Frank Gonzales, Detective, Cochise County Sheriff's Office He was a quiet and humble warrior in the war on drugs and a great partner.

T.J. "" Jimmy" Willson, Sheriff, Cochise County Sheriff's Office. An originator, a great sheriff, led the charge with his men on the drug traffickers before it became mainstream news.

Jimmy Judd, Sheriff, Cochise County Sheriff's Office. He was given the baton from Sheriff Willson and kept up the fight, a man of passion.

Frank Teachout, Narcotics Strike Force (Arizona Drug Control District) field supervisor A great leader and cop. He never knew how much he meant to me in my career.

Tomas "Tom" Riley, a crime reporter in Lake Havasu City, is an Irish transplant from Boston who became a confidant and good friend until his death. Tom was a great old-fashioned reporter who could dig up a story like no other.

Larry Reed, pastor and evangelist, is a former heroin addict and resident of San Quentin Prison in California. You saved my soul—the greatest gift a person can give. I was never able to thank you until now.

Neil Tietjen, Narcotics Strike Force, Tucson Field Supervisor. Our last telephone conversation before your eminent passing will forever be echoed in my memory. We knew the truth.

Bobby Griffith, Detective, Arizona Department of Public Safety. I carried on the prison gang assignment. You left us too early.

Mark Brown, Detective, Arizona Department of Public Safety (ADPS). I carried on the prison gang assignment. You left us too early.

Mike Vaugh, Detective, Los Angeles Police Department. A man's man. You watched my back and covered my six at the California Prison Gang Task Force (CPGTF) meetings.

Tony Casas, Deputy Chief, California Department of Corrections. I cherished the times we met. You inspired me and will always be great in my mind.

Robert 'Moco' Morrill, retired California Monterey Park Police Department. He retired from the Texas Department of Corrections and was a co-founder of the CPGTF. My story about you tells it all. I miss the laughter, friendship, and storytelling. I will share a bottle of red with your namesake.

Jim Brown, Sergeant Old Folsom Prison. You welcome me at the CPGTF meetings and twice at Old Folsom Prison. You shared with me legendary prison gang stories during your many years at Folsom Prison. You were the real deal, working in the trenches.

Lenny Lopez, Federal Bureau of Prisons, was a CPGTF board member. Lenny, you were one of a kind. Always upbeat and funny like no other.

Bill Whitlow, Detective AZDPS. Although I know, today, you would much prefer to be called a Trooper. My visit with you before your passing was very special to me. You will never be forgotten by the AZDPS brothers and sisters who knew you. I can hear a funny story coming up!

Armando "Mandi" Varela, you were a fierce soldier for the California Mexican Mafia prison gang in your day. Thank you for the 'schooling' you gave me and advice in working prison gangs. 'Mandi' I mentioned you in my manuscript because you accepted my humble reply, ' I need some schooling' when I met you. It became a valuable tool throughout the rest of my career. You were fierce and made it a point that I understood what you were telling me at the times we met. I hope in the end my actions and words 'schooled' you in ways that are external.